And You Thought You Knew Classic Movies!

Also by John DiLeo

Screen Savers II:
My Grab Bag of Classic Movies (2012)

Tennessee Williams and Company:
His Essential Screen Actors (2010)

Screen Savers:
40 Remarkable Movies Awaiting Rediscovery (2007)

100 Great Film Performances You Should
Remember—But Probably Don't (2002)

And You Thought You Knew Classic
Movies:
200 Quizzes for Golden Age Movie Lovers
(1999, 2013)

And You Thought You Knew Classic Movies!

200 Quizzes for Golden Age Movie Lovers

John DiLeo

HANSEN PUBLISHING GROUP

Cover photograph courtesy of Photofest. Rita Hayworth and Fred Astaire in *You Were Never Lovelier* (1942).

Hansen Publishing Group, LLC
302 Ryders Lane
East Brunswick, NJ 08816
http://hansenpublishing.com

Acknowledgments

Sincerest thanks to Naomi Wittes Reichstein, Cal Morgan, Anne Savarese, Richard Parks, Jerry Vermilye, Shira Levin, Randy Buck, Marty Jones, Clay Guthrie, Helen Silano, Julissa Santos, Alex Caliendo, Cynthia Sealy, Pauline Kael, Abby Hansen, my brother Michael, and my ever-patient partner, Earl McCarroll.

Colossal thanks to Maureen Caliendo.

In memory of dear, sweet Tony Razzano. He loved being thanked in my books, and I can never thank him enough.

Author's Note

I was born in 1961 and immediately went to the movies. I was raised on the musical blockbusters of the sixties (a mixed blessing) and thought that Julie Andrews was in *all* movies (which was fine with me). And yet, it was the old movies on television that truly entranced me. In the pre-VCR mid-seventies, I was the kid who set his alarm clock for 2 a.m. on school nights so I could get up and watch *To Each His Own* or *Words and Music*. The ushers got to know me by name when I saw *That's Entertainment!* thirteen times in the summer of 1974.

My grandmother once described the movies of her youth by saying, "They took you to another world." While today's movies are still capable of transporting us, the films of the Golden Age are generally more removed from life as we know it. Someone can watch *All About Eve* or *The Philadelphia Story* and say that people don't really talk like that, but wouldn't it be a more scintillating world if they did? I guess that sense of a heightened reality is what makes the period so hypnotic. Does color exist in nature the way it does in *Cover Girl*? Did you ever meet anyone like Garbo?

It was my parents and grandparents who first exposed me to everything from the toughest John Garfield picture to the frothiest Esther Williams extravaganza. Born on an Oscar night, my mother, Vera, would dress up to watch the Oscar telecasts when she was a teenager. I'd like to thank her and my father, John, for opening up this joyful and enriching world to a boy who continues to treasure it.

—John DiLeo

Table of Contents

Rules of the Game

This book covers movies up until the time I can remember going to them myself (mid to late sixties). I occasionally use more recent films, but only when there is a direct link to an older film or studio-system star.

The quizzes are organized by category rather than difficulty, so don't be discouraged if you find some of the early ones hard to finish (you may sail through later chapters).

There is no disrespect intended toward any favorites of yours that I may have neglected (*Casablanca* gets only two mentions). Certain films simply fit better into the quiz topics than others (you may end up thinking *Spellbound* is one of my favorites, but it isn't).

Each correct answer is worth one point. There are ten points to be had in each of the 200 quizzes. However, sprinkled throughout are 166 extra-credit questions where I ask for additional information, such as "Then name the film." So, a perfect score is actually 2166. Don't forget these extra points when you add up your total. You'll find the scoring key at the end.

—J.D.

One
Imitation of Life

1. Match the surprising first name (or nickname) of a screen character to the actress who played her.

    1. Billie C
    2. Butch J
    3. George H
    4. Stanley A
    5. Charlie E
    6. Frankie G
    7. Petey I
    8. Moe D
    9. Mike F
    10. Vinnie B

    a. Bette Davis in *In This Our Life*
    b. Irene Dunne in *Life with Father*
    c. Judy Holliday in *Born Yesterday*
    d. Thelma Ritter in *Pickup on South Street*
    e. Teresa Wright in *Shadow of a Doubt*
    f. Jane Russell in *Son of Paleface*
    g. Julie Harris in *The Member of the Wedding*
    h. Merle Oberon in *A Song to Remember*
    i. Ida Lupino in *The Man I Love*
    j. June Allyson in *The McConnell Story*

2.   Match the equally surprising first name (or nickname) of a screen
     character to the actor who played him.

1. Hot Lips	**a.** Joseph Cotten in *The Third Man*
2. Connie	**b.** Arthur Kennedy in *Champion*
3. Clare	**c.** Raymond Massey in *The Fountainhead*
4. Candy	**d.** Clark Gable in *The Misfits*
5. Holly	**e.** John Ireland in *Red River*
6. Laurie	**f.** Clifton Webb in *Sitting Pretty*
7. Gail	**g.** Clark Gable in *Honky Tonk*
8. Cherry	**h.** Bob Hope in *Road to Rio*
9. Gay	**i.** Peter Sellers in *Lolita*
10. Lynn	**j.** Peter Lawford in *Little Women*

3.   Match the title character to her last name.

1. *Laura*	**a.** Mundson
2. *Sabrina*	**b.** Clary
3. *Rebecca*	**c.** Hunt
4. *Gilda*	**d.** MacDuff
5. *Marnie*	**e.** De Winter
6. *Margie*	**f.** Johnson
7. *Lili*	**g.** Haze
8. *Desiree*	**h.** Fairchild
9. *Lolita*	**i.** Daurier
10. *Pinky*	**j.** Edgar

4.   Match the title character to his first name.

1. *Mr. Deeds Goes to Town*	**a.** Peter
2. *Mr. Smith Goes to Washington*	**b.** Longfellow
3. *Sullivan's Travels*	**c.** Cosmo
4. *Mister Roberts*	**d.** Henry
5. *Topper*	**e.** John
6. *Destry Rides Again*	**f.** Sam
7. *Dodsworth*	**g.** Alvin
8. *Frankenstein*	**h.** Jefferson
9. *Sergeant York*	**i.** Tom
10. *Captain Blood*	**j.** Doug

5.   Match the title character to the actress who played her.

1. *Nora Prentiss*	**a.** Jennifer Jones
2. *Ruby Gentry*	**b.** Jane Wyman
3. *Evelyn Prentice*	**c.** Ginger Rogers
4. *Letty Lynton*	**d.** Jean Simmons
5. *Lucy Gallant*	**e.** Ann Sheridan
6. *Alice Adams*	**f.** Joan Crawford
7. *Hilda Crane*	**g.** Myrna Loy
8. *Ann Vickers*	**h.** Irene Dunne
9. *Roxie Hart*	**i.** Miriam Hopkins
10. *Becky Sharp*	**j.** Katharine Hepburn

6. Match the title character to the actor who played him.

1. *Cass Timberlane*	**a.** Robert Taylor
2. *Lucky Jordan*	**b.** Gary Cooper
3. *Sorrowful Jones*	**c.** Fredric March
4. *Will Penny*	**d.** Alan Ladd
5. *Peter Ibbetson*	**e.** William Holden
6. *Boots Malone*	**f.** Bob Hope
7. *Bulldog Drummond*	**g.** Mickey Rooney
8. *Anthony Adverse*	**h.** Spencer Tracy
9. *Quentin Durward*	**i.** Ronald Colman
10. *Killer McCoy*	**j.** Charlton Heston

7. The title role is not always the starring role. Match the title character to the supporting actor who played him.

1. *Gunga Din* (starring Cary Grant)	**a.** Claude Rains
2. *Julius Caesar* (starring Marlon Brando)	**b.** Joseph Wiseman
3. *The Wizard of Oz* (starring Judy Garland)	**c.** Walter Slezak
4. *Dr. No* (starring Sean Connery)	**d.** Wayne Morris
5. *The Pirate* (starring Gene Kelly)	**e.** Louis Calhern
6. *The Thin Man* (starring William Powell)	**f.** Edward Ellis
7. *Topper* (starring Cary Grant)	**g.** Sam Jaffe
8. *Kid Galahad* (starring Edward G. Robinson)	**h.** Dean Jagger
9. *Brigham Young* (starring Tyrone Power)	**i.** Frank Morgan
10. *Here Comes Mr. Jordan* (starring Robert Montgomery)	**j.** Roland Young

8. Match the blissfully silly character name to the actress who played her.

1. Trudy Kockenlocker	**a.** Judy Holliday in *It Should Happen to You*
2. Luisa Ginglebusher	**b.** Barbara Stanwyck in *Ball of Fire*
3. Muzzy Van Hossmere	**c.** Margaret Sullavan in *The Good Fairy*
4. Gladys Glover	**d.** Ginger Rogers in *The Gay Divorcee*
5. Zelda Zanders	**e.** Carol Channing in *Thoroughly Modern Millie*
6. Sugarpuss O'Shea	**f.** Betty Garrett in *On the Town*
7. Phoebe Frost	**g.** Rita Moreno in *Singin' in the Rain*
8. Mimi Glossop	**h.** Betty Hutton in *The Miracle of Morgan's Creek*
9. Pola Debevoise	**i.** Jean Arthur in *A Foreign Affair*
10. Brunhilde Esterhazy	**j.** Marilyn Monroe in *How to Marry a Millionaire*

9. Match the swell-egant character name to the actor who played him. Don't you wish you had a name like one of these?

1. C. K. Dexter Haven	**a.** Zachary Scott in *Mildred Pierce*
2. Waldo Lydecker	**b.** Joe E. Brown in *Some Like It Hot*
3. Monte Beragon	**c.** Robert Walker in *Strangers on a Train*
4. Addison DeWitt	**d.** Clifton Webb in *Laura*
5. Bruno Anthony	**e.** Cary Grant in *An Affair to Remember*
6. J.J. Hunsecker	**f.** George Sanders in *All About Eve*
7. Osgood Fielding III	**g.** Vincent Price in *Laura*
8. Shelby Carpenter	**h.** Humphrey Bogart in *Sabrina*
9. Nickie Ferrante	**i.** Cary Grant in *The Philadelphia Story*
10. Linus Larrabee	**j.** Burt Lancaster in *Sweet Smell of Success*

10. Match the "Hitchcock blonde" character to the actress who played her.

1. Charlotte Inwood   **a.** Grace Kelly in *Dial M for Murder*
2. Margot Wendice   **b.** Grace Kelly in *Rear Window*
3. Gay Keane   **c.** Grace Kelly in *To Catch a Thief*
4. Jo McKenna   **d.** Janet Leigh in *Psycho*
5. Marion Crane   **e.** Tippi Hedren in *The Birds*
6. Judy Barton   **f.** Marlene Dietrich in *Stage Fright*
7. Lisa Fremont   **g.** Eva Marie Saint in *North by Northwest*
8. Eve Kendall   **h.** Ann Todd in *The Paradine Case*
9. Melanie Daniels   **i.** Kim Novak in *Vertigo*
10. Frances Stevens   **j.** Doris Day in *The Man Who Knew Too Much*

11. Match the western character to the actor who played him.

1. Waco Johnny Dean   **a.** John Wayne in *Stagecoach*
2. Johnny Ringo   **b.** Gregory Peck in *Duel in the Sun*
3. Jimmy Ringo   **c.** Dan Duryea in *Winchester '73*
4. The Ringo Kid   **d.** Gregory Peck in *The Gunfighter*
5. The Dancin' Kid   **e.** Gary Cooper in *High Noon*
6. Billy the Kid   **f.** Scott Brady in *Johnny Guitar*
7. Kid Shelleen   **g.** John Wayne in *The Searchers*
8. Lewt McCanles   **h.** John Ireland in *Gunfight at the O.K. Corral*
9. Ethan Edwards   **i.** Paul Newman in *The Left Handed Gun*
10. Will Kane   **j.** Lee Marvin in *Cat Ballou*

12.   Match the Tennessee Williams character to the performer who
      played him/her on the screen. Then name the film.

1. Laura Wingfield	a. Vivien Leigh
2. Catherine Holly	b. Ava Gardner
3. Carol Cutrere	c. Anna Magnani
4. Karen Stone	d. Jane Wyman
5. Lady Torrance	e. Geraldine Page
6. Hannah Jelkes	f. Joanne Woodward
7. Maxine Faulk	g. Noel Coward
8. Heavenly Finley	h. Elizabeth Taylor
9. Alexandra Del Lago	i. Shirley Knight
10. The Witch of Capri	j. Deborah Kerr

13.   Match the "Johnny" character to the actor who played him.

1. Johnny Friendly	a. Sterling Hayden in *Johnny Guitar*
2. Johnnie Gray	b. Cary Grant in *Suspicion*
3. Johnnie Aysgarth	c. Edward G. Robinson in *Key Largo*
4. Johnny Case	d. Don Murray in *A Hatful of Rain*
5. Johnny Farrell	e. Lee J. Cobb in *On the Waterfront*
6. Johnny Logan	f. James Mason in *Odd Man Out*
7. Johnny Pope	g. Glenn Ford in *Gilda*
8. Johnny Nolan	h. Buster Keaton in *The General*
9. Johnny Rocco	i. James Dunn in *A Tree Grows in Brooklyn*
10. Johnny McQueen	j. Cary Grant in *Holiday*

14.   Match the real person to the actress who played her on the screen (in the year listed by her name). Name the films too.

1. Emily Brontë	a. Susan Hayward (1958)
2. Dolly Madison	b. Deborah Kerr (1959)
3. Sheilah Graham	c. Jean Arthur (1936)
4. Barbara Graham	d. Greer Garson (1960)
5. Elizabeth I	e. Ida Lupino (1946)
6. Elizabeth Kenny	f. Myrna Loy (1936)
7. Elizabeth Barrett Browning	g. Jean Simmons (1953)
8. Billie Burke	h. Jennifer Jones (1957)
9. Calamity Jane	i. Ginger Rogers (1946)
10. Eleanor Roosevelt	j. Rosalind Russell (1946)

15.   Match the real person to the actor who played him on the screen (in the year listed by his name). Name the films too.

1. Andrew Jackson	a. Paul Muni (1939)
2. Rembrandt	b. Fredric March (1944)
3. Thomas Alva Edison	c. Wallace Beery (1934)
4. Dr. Paul Ehrlich	d. Charles Laughton (1936)
5. Benito Juarez	e. Edward G. Robinson (1940)
6. Pancho Villa	f. David Niven (1946)
7. Charles Lindbergh	g. Lionel Barrymore (1936)
8. Mark Twain	h. James Stewart (1957)
9. Ernie Pyle	i. Burgess Meredith (1945)
10. Aaron Burr	j. Spencer Tracy (1940)

16. Some characters are talked about a great deal without actually appearing. They may be seen in photographs or even heard on the soundtrack. Some of them are just plain dead. Match each character to the film in which he/she is important to the story but remains unseen.

1. Claude Daigle	a. *Laura*
2. Tina Mara	b. *A Letter to Three Wives*
3. Stephen Haines	c. *The King and I*
4. Addie Ross	d. *The Philadelphia Story*
5. Tim Hilton	e. *A Streetcar Named Desire*
6. Diane Redfern	f. *The Maltese Falcon* (1941)
7. Shep Huntleigh	g. *The Women*
8. Tom Leonowens	h. *The Bad Seed*
9. Floyd Thursby	i. *The Miracle of Morgan's Creek*
10. Private Ratzkiwatzki	j. *Since You Went Away*

17. Match the clownish character name to the man who played him.

1. Rufus T. Firefly	a. W.C. Fields in *My Little Chickadee*
2. Julius Kelp	b. Red Skelton in *Neptune's Daughter*
3. Jack Spratt	c. Sterling Hayden in *Dr. Strangelove*
4. Egbert Sousé	d. Groucho Marx in *A Night at the Opera*
5. Jack D. Ripper	e. Jerry Lewis in *The Nutty Professor*
6. Buzzy Bellew	f. Charlie Chaplin in *The Great Dictator*
7. Cuthbert J. Twillie	g. Jerry Lewis in *Scared Stiff*
8. Adenoid Hynkel	h. Groucho Marx in *Duck Soup*
9. Otis P. Driftwood	i. Danny Kaye in *Wonder Man*
10. Myron Myron Mertz	j. W.C. Fields in *The Bank Dick*

18. Sometimes a character is known by two different names over the
     course of one movie. Whatever the reason (career move, amnesia,
     undercover work, etc.), it usually leads to complications. Match the
     double-named character to the film in which he/she appears.

1. Anthony Edwardes/ John Ballantine   **a.** *Lady for a Day*

2. Ethel Whitehead/ Lorna Hansen   **b.** *Twentieth Century*
   Forbes

3. Joe Pendleton/ Bruce Farnsworth   **c.** *Midnight*

4. Mildred Plotka/ Lily Garland   **d.** *The Damned Don't Cry*

5. Brad Allen/ Rex Stetson   **e.** *Spellbound*

6. Eve Peabody/ Baroness Czerny   **f.** *Mr. Deeds Goes to Town*

7. Apple Annie/ Mrs. E. Worthington   **g.** *The Palm Beach Story*
   Manville

8. Tom Jeffers/ Captain McGloo   **h.** *Pillow Talk*

9. Babe Bennett/ Mary Dawson   **i.** *Here Comes Mr. Jordan*

10. Johnny Jones/ Huntley Haverstock   **j.** *Foreign Correspondent*

19. It's always a jolt when there is a character in an old movie with a
     name that would become famous in the years since the film was
     made. Match each character to the actor who played him.

1. Gig Young   **a.** Edward G. Robinson in *Scarlet Street*

2. Steve Martin   **b.** Cesar Romero in *The Thin Man*

3. Oliver Stone   **c.** William Demarest in *The Jolson Story*

4. Oliver Reed   **d.** George Nader in *The Female Animal*

5. Chris Farley   **e.** Humphrey Bogart in *To Have and
                            Have Not*

6. John Kennedy   **f.** Kent Smith in *Cat People*

7. Harry Morgan   **g.** Gig Young in *The Gay Sisters*

8. Christopher Cross   **h.** Walter Connolly in *Nothing Sacred*

9. Chris Jorgenson   **i.** Paul Newman in *What a Way to Go!*

10. Larry Flint   **j.** Dick Powell in *The Tall Target*

20.   You remember the face, you remember the scenes, but do you remember the performer's name? Pick the performer on the right who played each of the unforgettable roles on the left.

1. "Teddy Roosevelt" Brewster in *Arsenic and Old Lace*
a. John Alexander; **b.** Jerry Colonna; **c.** Walter Abel; **d.** Allyn Joslyn

2. Lina Lamont in *Singin' in the Rain*
a. Jan Sterling; **b.** Barbara Nichols; **c.** Jean Hagen; **d.** Jane Greer

3. Countess De Lave in *The Women*
a. Laura Hope Crews; **b.** Billie Burke; **c.** Constance Bennett; **d.** Mary Boland

4. Maggie Prescott in *Funny Face*
a. Dolores Gray; **b.** Kay Thompson; **c.** Nina Foch; **d.** Janis Paige

5. Mrs. Van Hopper in *Rebecca*
a. Ilka Chase; **b.** Florence Bates; **c.** Lucile Watson; **d.** Constance Collier

6. Madame Defarge in *A Tale of Two Cities*
a. Blanche Yurka; **b.** Alla Nazimova; **c.** Katina Paxinou; **d.** Maria Ouspenskaya

7. Jeffrey Cordova in *The Band Wagon*
a. Georges Guetary; **b.** Hans Conried; **c.** Anton Walbrook; **d.** Jack Buchanan

8. Lady Catherine de Bourgh in *Pride and Prejudice*
a. May Whitty; **b.** Marie Dressler; **c.** Edith Evans; **d.** Edna May Oliver

9. Vera Charles in *Auntie Mame*
a. Kay Walsh; **b.** Coral Browne; **c.** Pamela Brown; **d.** Joan Greenwood

10. Belle Watling in *Gone With the Wind*
a. Ina Claire; **b.** Osa Massen; **c.** Ona Munson; **d.** Claire Trevor

Two

Family Plot

21. Match the actress to the film in which she played a mother.

1. Spring Byington	**a.** *Citizen Kane*
2. Anne Revere	**b.** *Gone With the Wind*
3. Beulah Bondi	**c.** *Mutiny on the Bounty* (1935)
4. Agnes Moorehead	**d.** *White Heat*
5. Jo Van Fleet	**e.** *Dead End*
6. Margaret Wycherly	**f.** *Our Town*
7. Barbara O'Neil	**g.** *My Man Godfrey* (1936)
8. Marjorie Main	**h.** *A Place in the Sun*
9. Alice Brady	**i.** *Kitty Foyle*
10. Gladys Cooper	**j.** *I'll Cry Tomorrow*

22. Match the actor to the film in which he played a father.

1. Frank Morgan	a. *Johnny Belinda*
2. Donald Crisp	b. *Pride and Prejudice*
3. Thomas Mitchell	c. *How Green Was My Valley*
4. Charles Bickford	d. *My Darling Clementine*
5. Samuel S. Hinds	e. *The Mortal Storm*
6. Edmund Gwenn	f. *It Happened One Night*
7. Claude Rains	g. *The Furies*
8. Walter Connolly	h. *Gone With the Wind*
9. Walter Huston	i. *Kings Row*
10. Walter Brennan	j. *It's a Wonderful Life*

23. Match the child actress to the film in which she appeared.

1. Natalie Wood	a. *The Keys of the Kingdom*
2. Elizabeth Taylor	b. *The Bad Seed*
3. Margaret O'Brien	c. *The White Cliffs of Dover*
4. Peggy Ann Garner	d. *Gone With the Wind*
5. Bonita Granville	e. *These Three*
6. Patty McCormack	f. *The Philadelphia Story*
7. Cammie King	g. *To Kill a Mockingbird*
8. Patty Duke	h. *The Ghost and Mrs. Muir*
9. Mary Badham	i. *The Goddess*
10. Virginia Weidler	j. *Our Vines Have Tender Grapes*

24. Match the child actor to the film in which he appeared.

1. Freddie Bartholomew   a. *Gentleman's Agreement*
2. Scotty Beckett   b. *The Champ* (1931)
3. Jackie Cooper   c. *National Velvet*
4. Darryl Hickman   d. *Beau Geste* (1939)
5. Dean Stockwell   e. *Anna Karenina* (1935)
6. Donald O'Connor   f. *Tarzan Finds a Son!*
7. Roddy McDowall   g. *The Yearling*
8. Johnny Sheffield   h. *Kings Row*
9. Jackie "Butch" Jenkins   i. *The Pied Piper*
10. Claude Jarman, Jr.   j. *Leave Her to Heaven*

25. Match the actress to the aunt she played on the screen (in the year listed by her name). How about naming the films too?

1. Agnes Moorehead (1942)   a. Aunt Abby
2. Fay Bainter (1938)   b. Aunt March
3. Clara Blandick (1939)   c. Aunt Lavinia
4. Josephine Hull (1944)   d. Aunt Fanny
5. Joan Blondell (1945)   e. Aunt Birdie
6. Miriam Hopkins (1949)   f. Aunt Pittypat
7. Patricia Collinge (1941)   g. Aunt Belle
8. Edna May Oliver (1933)   h. Aunt Sissy
9. Laura Hope Crews (1939)   i. Aunt Eller
10. Charlotte Greenwood (1955) j. Aunt Em

26.   Match the fictional family to the film that tells their story.

1. The Stephensons	**a.** *Seven Brides for Seven Brothers*
2. The Morgans	**b.** *Meet Me in St. Louis*
3. The Pontipees	**c.** *Shane*
4. The Benedicts	**d.** *National Velvet*
5. The Sycamores	**e.** *The Best Years of Our Lives*
6. The Starretts	**f.** *Giant*
7. The Baxters	**g.** *How Green Was My Valley*
8. The Browns	**h.** *My Man Godfrey*
9. The Bullocks	**i.** *The Yearling*
10. The Smiths	**j.** *You Can't Take It With You*

27.   Match the first names of two performers with the same last name to the film in which they both appeared. Some of the pairs are related and some are not.

1. Kirk and Paul	**a.** *Tea and Sympathy*
2. James and Paul	**b.** *Night Flight*
3. James and Jeanne	**c.** *The V.I.P.s*
4. Hayley and John	**d.** *Carbine Williams*
5. Deborah and John	**e.** *The Chalk Garden*
6. Lionel and John	**f.** *The Time of Your Life*
7. Elizabeth and Robert	**g.** *The Proud Rebel*
8. Elizabeth and Rod	**h.** *Conspirator*
9. Alan and David	**i.** *A Letter to Three Wives*
10. Bette and James	**j.** *Winter Meeting*

28. Match the performer to the film in which he/she is related to Shirley Temple.

1. Gary Cooper (her father)
2. Joel McCrea (her father)
3. Henry Fonda (her father)
4. Ginger Rogers (her cousin)
5. Myrna Loy (her sister)
6. Lionel Barrymore (her grandfather)
7. Jean Hersholt (her grandfather)
8. C. Aubrey Smith (her grandfather)
9. Claire Trevor (her mother)
10. Claudette Colbert (her mother)

a. *Baby Take a Bow*
b. *Since You Went Away*
c. *Now and Forever*
d. *Fort Apache*
e. *Wee Willie Winkie*
f. *The Little Colonel*
g. *I'll Be Seeing You*
h. *Heidi*
i. *Our Little Girl*
j. *The Bachelor and the Bobby-Soxer*

29. Match the performer to the film in which he/she is related to Judy Garland.

1. Gloria DeHaven (her sister)
2. Charley Grapewin (her uncle)
3. Gladys Cooper (her aunt)
4. Robert Walker (her husband)
5. Stuart Erwin (her brother)
6. Billie Burke (her mother)
7. George Murphy (her father)
8. Liza Minnelli (her daughter)
9. Nancy Walker (her cousin)
10. Leon Ames (her father)

a. *The Pirate*
b. *Everybody Sing*
c. *Meet Me in St. Louis*
d. *The Clock*
e. *In the Good Old Summertime*
f. *Summer Stock*
g. *Pigskin Parade*
h. *Girl Crazy*
i. *The Wizard of Oz*
j. *Little Nellie Kelly*

30.   Match the performer to the film in which he/she is related to Elizabeth Taylor.

1. Donald Crisp (her father)   a. *Little Women*

2. Carroll Baker (her daughter)   b. *The Last Time I Saw Paris*

3. Donna Reed (her sister)   c. *Suddenly, Last Summer*

4. Janet Leigh (her sister)   d. *Butterfield 8*

5. Jack Carson (her brother-in-law)   e. *A Place in the Sun*

6. Mildred Dunnock (her mother)   f. *National Velvet*

7. Billie Burke (her mother-in-law)   g. *Lassie Come Home*

8. Mercedes McCambridge (her   h. *Cat on a Hot Tin Roof*
   mother)

9. Shepperd Strudwick (her father)   i. *Giant*

10. Nigel Bruce (her grandfather)   j. *Father's Little Dividend*

31.   Sisters Olivia de Havilland and Joan Fontaine worked with some of the same actors. The first film in each pair features Fontaine and the second features de Havilland. Match the pair of films to the actor who appeared in both of them.

1. *The Constant Nymph/ Hold Back the Dawn*   a. Joseph Cotten

2. *September Affair/ Hush ... Hush, Sweet Charlotte*   b. Mark Stevens

3. *Something to Live For/ The Well-Groomed Bride*   c. John Lund

4. *Darling, How Could You!/ To Each His Own*   d. Ray Milland

5. *From This Day Forward/ The Snake Pit*   e. Charles Boyer

6. *Frenchman's Creek/ Captain Blood*   f. Rossano Brazzi

7. *The Affairs of Susan/ In This Our Life*   g. Patric Knowles

8. *Serenade/ The Private Lives of Elizabeth and Essex*   h. George Brent

9. *A Certain Smile/ Light in the Piazza*   i. Vincent Price

10. *Ivy/ The Charge of the Light Brigade*   j. Basil Rathbone

32.   Henry and Jane Fonda may have been from different generations, but they still managed to work with some of the same performers. The first film in each pair features Henry and the second features Jane. Match each pair of films to the performer who appeared in both of them. Some of these films are all-star affairs and the Fondas don't always share actual screen time with each performer.

1. *The Best Man/ Sunday in New York*

2. *Once Upon a Time in the West/ Any Wednesday*

3. *Mister Roberts/ The China Syndrome*

4. *Tales of Manhattan/ Barefoot in the Park*

5. *You Belong to Me/ Walk on the Wild Side*

6. *Advise and Consent/ Hurry Sundown*

7. *Ash Wednesday/ The Blue Bird*

8. *The Tin Star/ Tall Story*

9. *12 Angry Men/ The Chase*

10. *Sex and the Single Girl/ Cat Ballou*

a. Jack Lemmon

b. Elizabeth Taylor

c. Barbara Stanwyck

d. Anthony Perkins

e. Stubby Kaye

f. Jason Robards

g. Cliff Robertson

h. Charles Boyer

i. E.G. Marshall

j. Burgess Meredith

Three
This Land Is Mine

33. Match the actor to the king he played in a film (in the year listed by his name). Grab some extra credit and name the films.

1. Claude Rains (1938)
2. Rex Harrison (1946)
3. Wallace Beery (1922)
4. George Sanders (1947 and 1955)
5. Frank Morgan (1948)
6. Basil Rathbone (1939)
7. Mel Ferrer (1953)
8. Robert Morley (1938)
9. Peter O'Toole (1964 and 1968)
10. Laurence Olivier (1944)

a. Charles II
b. Richard the Lionhearted
c. Louis XVI
d. Richard III
e. King of Siam
f. Henry II
g. Louis XIII
h. Henry V
i. King John
j. King Arthur

34.   Match the actress to the queen she played in a film (in the year listed by her name). And while you're at it, name the films, too.

1. Deborah Kerr (1953)

2. Viveca Lindfors (1948)

3. Katharine Hepburn (1968)

4. Judith Anderson (1953)

5. Ethel Barrymore (1932)

6. Flora Robson (1937 and 1940)

7. Ava Gardner (1953)

8. Merle Oberon (1933)

9. Irene Dunne (1950)

10. Angela Lansbury (1948)

a. Queen Herodias

b. Queen Elizabeth I

c. Queen Anne of France

d. Catherine Parr

e. Empress Alexandra

f. Anne Boleyn

g. Queen Margaret of Spain

h. Queen Victoria

i. Eleanor of Aquitaine

j. Queen Guinevere

35.   Match the piece of real estate to the film in which it appears.

1. Spanish Bit

2. Twelve Oaks

3. Reata

4. Peckerwood

5. Gull Cottage

6. Xanadu

7. Cascade

8. Green Manors

9. Back of the Moon

10. Manderley

a. *Gone With the Wind*

b. *Duel in the Sun*

c. *Citizen Kane*

d. *The Ghost and Mrs. Muir*

e. *Spellbound*

f. *Leave Her to Heaven*

g. *Giant*

h. *Rebecca*

i. *Now, Voyager*

j. *Auntie Mame*

36. Match the first name (or nickname) of a screen character to the performer who played it.

1. Kansas	**a.** Betty Hutton in *Incendiary Blonde*
2. Dallas	**b.** Shirley Temple in *Fort Apache*
3. Texas	**c.** Olivia de avilland in *The Snake Pit*
4. Georgia	**d.** Ricky Nelson in *Rio Bravo*
5. Virginia	**e.** Glenda Farrell in *Lady for a Day*
6. Nevada	**f.** Sonny Tufts in *So Proudly We Hail!*
7. Missouri	**g.** Dorothy Lamour in *Chad Hanna*
8. Colorado	**h.** Lana Turner in *The Bad and the Beautiful*
9. Albany	**i.** Alan Ladd in *The Carpetbaggers*
10. Philadelphia	**j.** Claire Trevor in *Stagecoach*

37. Match the film to the city in which it is primarily set.

1. *Double Indemnity*	**a.** San Francisco
2. *The Third Man*	**b.** Berlin
3. *The Shop Around the Corner*	**c.** Los Angeles
4. *Born Yesterday*	**d.** New York
5. *Vertigo*	**e.** Vienna
6. *The Heiress*	**f.** Washington, D.C.
7. *Ninotchka*	**g.** London
8. *Notorious*	**h.** Rio de Janeiro
9. *Gaslight*	**i.** Budapest
10. *One, Two, Three*	**j.** Paris

38.   Match the film to the country in which it is primarily set.

1. *Johnny Belinda*	**a.** China
2. *The Keys of the Kingdom*	**b.** Sweden
3. *On the Beach*	**c.** U.S.A.
4. *Gilda*	**d.** Spain
5. *I Remember Mama*	**e.** Australia
6. *Hold Back the Dawn*	**f.** France
7. *All This, and Heaven Too*	**g.** Turkey
8. *Queen Christina*	**h.** Argentina
9. *America, America*	**i.** Mexico
10. *For Whom the Bell Tolls*	**j.** Canada

39.   Match the film about World War II (or the years leading up to it) to the country in which it is primarily set.

1. *The Diary of Anne Frank*	**a.** Burma
2. *To Be or Not to Be*	**b.** Germany
3. *The Seventh Cross*	**c.** U.S.A.
4. *Mrs. Miniver*	**d.** Italy
5. *The Hasty Heart*	**e.** Japan
6. *A Walk in the Sun*	**f.** Holland
7. *5 Fingers*	**g.** England
8. *The North Star*	**h.** Russia
9. *The Purple Heart*	**i.** Poland
10. *Watch on the Rhine*	**j.** Turkey

40. Many actors put movie stardom on hold to serve in World War II. When they returned, the Hollywood publicity machine made much of their comeback vehicles. Match the actor to his first post-WWII film. As you can see, some fared far better than others.

1. Robert Taylor	a. *The Razor's Edge*
2. Clark Gable	b. *The Strange Love of Martha Ivers*
3. Van Heflin	c. *The Dark Mirror*
4. Robert Montgomery	d. *Adventure*
5. William Holden	e. *Sinbad the Sailor*
6. Tyrone Power	f. *They Were Expendable*
7. Douglas Fairbanks, Jr.	g. *Wild Harvest*
8. Victor Mature	h. *Blaze of Noon*
9. Robert Preston	i. *Undercurrent*
10. Lew Ayres	j. *My Darling Clementine*

41. Match the exotic film title to one of its stars.

1. *Istanbul*	a. Alan Ladd
2. *Macao*	b. Maria Montez
3. *Sudan*	c. Tyrone Power
4. *Honolulu*	d. Jeanette MacDonald
5. *Cairo*	e. Errol Flynn
6. *Calcutta*	f. Maureen O'Hara
7. *Suez*	g. Charles Boyer
8. *Malaya*	h. Jane Russell
9. *Bagdad*	i. Spencer Tracy
10. *Algiers*	j. Eleanor Powell

42.   Match the performer to his/her place of birth.

1. Errol Flynn	**a.** Japan
2. Raymond Massey	**b.** U.S.A.
3. Vivien Leigh	**c.** England
4. Olivia de Havilland	**d.** Canada
5. Louis Hayward	**e.** Russia
6. Deborah Kerr	**f.** Tasmania
7. Bob Hope	**g.** Belgium
8. George Sanders	**h.** South Africa
9. Audrey Hepburn	**i.** India
10. Fred Astaire	**j.** Scotland

Four

Career

43. Match the star to the film in which he/she made an early (and very brief) screen appearance.

1. Audrey Hepburn	a. *Criss Cross*
2. Alan Ladd	b. *Top Hat*
3. Tony Curtis	c. *Since You Went Away*
4. James Dean	d. *Has Anybody Seen My Gal*
5. David Niven	e. *Citizen Kane*
6. Gary Cooper	f. *Gentleman's Agreement*
7. Myrna Loy	g. *The Lavender Hill Mob*
8. Lucille Ball	h. *Rose Marie* (1936)
9. Dorothy Dandridge	i. *Wings*
10. Gene Nelson	j. *The Jazz Singer* (1927)

44. Match the star to the film from a popular series in which he/she appeared.

1. Jeanette MacDonald	a. *Andy Hardy's Double Life*
2. John Barrymore	b. *Blondie on a Budget*
3. Esther Williams	c. *Maisie Goes to Reno*
4. Lana Turner	d. *Calling Dr. Kildare*
5. Anthony Quinn	e. *The Sun Comes Up* (Lassie film)
6. Rita Hayworth	f. *The Adventures of Sherlock Holmes*
7. Ava Gardner	g. *Charlie Chan in London*
8. James Stewart	h. *Bulldog Drummond's Revenge*
9. Ida Lupino	i. *After the Thin Man*
10. Ray Milland	j. *Road to Morocco*

45. Match the star to the famous film in which he/she had a supporting role.

1. Humphrey Bogart	a. *The Best Years of Our Lives*
2. Susan Hayward	b. *Winchester '73*
3. Rock Hudson	c. *Life with Father*
4. Joan Fontaine	d. *Out of the Past*
5. Mickey Rooney	e. *Captains Courageous*
6. Virginia Mayo	f. *Gunga Din*
7. Elizabeth Taylor	g. *Beau Geste* (1939)
8. Natalie Wood	h. *The Ox-Bow Incident*
9. Kirk Douglas	i. *The Searchers*
10. Anthony Quinn	j. *Dark Victory*

46. Match the not-so-famous performer to the very famous film in which he/she starred or at least played a very important role.

1. Barbara Parkins   **a.** *Guess Who's Coming to Dinner*

2. Tom Tryon   **b.** *Peyton Place*

3. Dorothy Comingore   **c.** *East of Eden*

4. Richard Davalos   **d.** *King Kong* (1933)

5. Millie Perkins   **e.** *Citizen Kane*

6. Virginia Cherrill   **f.** *Valley of the Dolls*

7. Katharine Houghton   **g.** *The Broadway Melody*

8. Charles King   **h.** *City Lights*

9. Robert Armstrong   **i.** *The Cardinal*

10. Lee Philips   **j.** *The Diary of Anne Frank*

47. Following each famous film, I have listed the actor most associated with it. However, these actors were not necessarily the stars of these films. Match each film to the actor who is the top-billed male in its opening credits.

1. *The Bridge on the River Kwai* -Alec Guinness   **a.** Joel McCrea

2. *Flying Down to Rio* -Fred Astaire   **b.** Robert Young

3. *This Gun for Hire* -Alan Ladd   **c.** George Sanders

4. *Frankenstein* -Boris Karloff   **d.** William Holden

5. *Dead End* -Humphrey Bogart   **e.** Colin Clive

6. *Kind Hearts and Coronets* -Alec Guinness   **f.** Claude Rains

7. *Crossfire* -Robert Ryan   **g.** Robert Preston

8. *Miracle on 34th Street* -Edmund Gwenn   **h.** Dennis Price

9. *Four Daughters* -John Garfield   **i.** Gene Raymond

10. *The Picture of Dorian Gray* -Hurd Hatfield   **j.** John Payne

48.   Hollywood was always looking for the next Greta Garbo or Marlene Dietrich. Sometimes they found one (Ingrid Bergman), but most often they didn't. Match the European actress to one of the films that failed to make her a Hollywood star.

1. Elissa Landi
2. Bella Darvi
3. Franciska Gaal
4. Anna Sten
5. Signe Hasso
6. Alida Valli
7. Mai Zetterling
8. Cornell Borchers
9. Marta Toren
10. Hildegarde Neff

a. *The Buccaneer* (1938)
b. *Sirocco*
c. *The Paradine Case*
d. *The Egyptian*
e. *The Sign of the Cross*
f. *The Snows of Kilimanjaro*
g. *The House on 92nd Street*
h. *The Big Lift*
i. *The Wedding Night*
j. *Knock on Wood*

49.   Match the actor to the role that made him a star. Then name the film.

1. James Cagney
2. Kirk Douglas
3. John Garfield
4. Alan Ladd
5. William Holden
6. Burt Lancaster
7. Humphrey Bogart
8. Richard Widmark
9. James Dean
10. Warren Beatty

a. Tommy Udo
b. Joe Bonaparte
c. Cal Trask
d. Mickey Borden
e. Roy Earle
f. Bud Stamper
g. The Swede
h. Tom Powers
i. Raven
j. Midge Kelly

50. Match the actress to the role that made her a star. Then name the film.

1. Lauren Bacall   **a.** Marie Browning
2. Jane Russell   **b.** Ulah
3. Kim Novak   **c.** Kitty Collins
4. Ava Gardner   **d.** Lady Lou
5. Greer Garson   **e.** Anita Hoffman
6. Rita Hayworth   **f.** Katherine Chipping
7. Dorothy Lamour   **g.** Rose Loomis
8. Ingrid Bergman   **h.** Madge Owens
9. Mae West   **i.** Dona Sol
10. Marilyn Monroe   **j.** Rio

51. Match the star to the horror film or thriller in which he/she appeared in the twilight of his/her screen career.

1. Joan Crawford   **a.** *The Day of the Triffids*
2. Bette Davis   **b.** *The Night Walker*
3. Herbert Marshall   **c.** *Trog*
4. Dana Andrews   **d.** *The Fly* (1958)
5. Barbara Stanwyck   **e.** *Die! Die! My Darling!*
6. Howard Keel   **f.** *Burnt Offerings*
7. Joan Fontaine   **g.** *Lady in a Cage*
8. Tallulah Bankhead   **h.** *The Devil's Own* (1967)
9. Ray Milland   **i.** *Curse of the Demon*
10. Olivia de Havilland   **j.** *The Thing with Two Heads*

52.   Match the "Golden Age" performer to the relatively recent film in which he/she appeared.

1. Sylvia Sidney	a. *Hannah and Her Sisters*
2. Gloria Grahame	b. *Misery*
3. Van Johnson	c. *The Shawshank Redemption*
4. Lloyd Nolan	d. *Dangerous Liaisons*
5. James Whitmore	e. *Melvin and Howard*
6. Mildred Natwick	f. *The Age of Innocence*
7. Dorothy Malone	g. *Edward Scissorhands*
8. Alexis Smith	h. *The Purple Rose of Cairo*
9. Lauren Bacall	i. *Beetlejuice*
10. Vincent Price	j. *Basic Instinct*

53.   Match the star to the year in which he/she died.

1. John Garfield	a. 1937
2. Montgomery Clift	b. 1942
3. Carole Lombard	c. 1946
4. Betty Grable	d. 1952
5. Jean Harlow	e. 1957
6. W.C. Fields	f. 1961
7. Joan Crawford	g. 1966
8. Gary Cooper	h. 1969
9. Humphrey Bogart	i. 1973
10. Judy Garland	j. 1977

Five

Who Was That Lady?

Hint: Each star has 5 correct answers.

54. Greta Garbo or Lillian Gish?

1. Who won the first N.Y. Film Critics Award for Best Actress?
2. Who starred with Ronald Colman in *The White Sister?*
3. Who starred with John Gilbert in *La Bohème?*
4. Who was in a film directed by Charles Laughton?
5. Who starred in *Love* (a silent version of *Anna Karenina*)?
6. Who was in *Commandos Strike at Dawn* with Paul Muni?
7. Who starred with Herbert Marshall in *The Painted Veil?*
8. Who received an Oscar nomination for her first talkie?
9. Who received a 1954 honorary Oscar?
10. Who received a 1970 honorary Oscar?

55.   Greer Garson or Norma Shearer?

1. Who played Elizabeth Barrett Browning?
2. Who played Jane Austen's Elizabeth Bennet?
3. Whose last MGM film was *Her Cardboard Lover*?
4. Who appeared in a Shakespeare film directed by George Cukor?
5. Who appeared in a Shakespeare film directed by Joseph L. Mankiewicz?
6. Who starred in a sequel to the movie that won her an Oscar?
7. Who starred with Robert Taylor in *Escape*?
8. Who received five consecutive Best Actress Oscar nominations?
9. Who starred as Amanda in *Private Lives*?
10. Who co-starred with Joan Crawford in *When Ladies Meet*?

56.   Joan Crawford or Bette Davis?

1. Who became a star in the silent era?
2. Who played Mildred in a 1934 John Cromwell film?
3. Who starred in an Otto Preminger film with Henry Fonda?
4. Who starred in a 1948 comedy with Robert Montgomery?
5. Who sang and danced in *Thank Your Lucky Stars*?
6. Who won the 1945 Best Actress Oscar?
7. Who played *Sadie McKee* and *Harriet Craig*?
8. Who starred as one of *The Sisters* in 1938?
9. Whose first film was *Bad Sister*?
10. Who played a 1937 Gertrude Lawrence stage role in a 1940 film?

57. Jean Arthur or Carole Lombard?

1. Who got to choose between Melvyn Douglas and Fred MacMurray in *Too Many Husbands*?

2. Who got caught between Cary Grant and Kay Francis in *In Name Only*?

3. Who played a dedicated nurse in *Vigil in the Night*?

4. Who starred as *The Ex-Mrs. Bradford* with William Powell?

5. Who starred in a 1941 Alfred Hitchcock comedy?

6. Who starred with Edward G. Robinson in a 1935 John Ford comedy?

7. Who was stranded on an island with Bing Crosby in *We're Not Dressing*?

8. Who played James Stewart's bride in *Made for Each Other*?

9. Who starred with John Wayne in *A Lady Takes a Chance*?

10. Who starred with Charles Boyer in *History Is Made at Night*?

58. Ida Lupino or Barbara Stanwyck?

1. Who was never nominated for a Best Actress Oscar?

2. Who starred in *Gambling Lady* and *The Lady Gambles*?

3. Who was one of *The Gay Sisters* in 1942?

4. Who was the unhappy farm girl transformed by love in *Deep Valley*?

5. Who starred with Errol Flynn in *Cry Wolf*?

6. Who married Humphrey Bogart in *The Two Mrs. Carrolls*?

7. Who sang and danced with Olivia de Havilland in *Thank Your Lucky Stars*?

8. Who made two films with Clark Gable?

9. Who was the superintendent of 1955's *Women's Prison*?

10. Who starred in the murder melodrama *Ladies in Retirement*?

59.   Alice Faye or Jeanette MacDonald?

1. Who starred in the musical remake of *Smilin' Through*?
2. Who was *The Girl of the Golden West*?
3. Who made an early appearance with Spencer Tracy in *Now I'll Tell*?
4. Who starred in a 1942 film of a Rodgers and Hart musical fantasy?
5. Who starred in a 1940 film of a Noel Coward musical?
6. Who played Belle in a film about an 1871 disaster?
7. Who sang "This Year's Kisses" in *On the Avenue*?
8. Who made an attempt at film noir in *Fallen Angel*?
9. Who played Jane Powell's mother in *Three Daring Daughters*?
10. Who made a comeback as the mother in the 1962 *State Fair*?

60.   Olivia de Havilland or Joan Fontaine?

1. Who was one of *The Women*?
2. Who starred with Brian Aherne in *The Great Garrick*?
3. Who starred in a 1952 adaptation of a Daphne du Maurier novel?
4. Who starred as Charlotte Brontë in *Devotion*?
5. Who appeared in a film version of a Shakespeare comedy?
6. Who was directed by Ida Lupino in *The Bigamist*?
7. Who appeared with Myrna Loy in *The Ambassador's Daughter*?
8. Who starred in *Island in the Sun* with Harry Belafonte?
9. Who was one of Fred Astaire's dance partners?
10. Whose list of leading men includes both Bing Crosby and Mario Lanza?

61. Jane Wyman or Loretta Young?

  1. Who played Mrs. Will Rogers in *The Story of Will Rogers*?

  2. Who starred in a 1950 Alfred Hitchcock thriller?

  3. Who starred in a 1946 Orson Welles thriller?

  4. Who starred in the 1949 comedy *Mother Is a Freshman*?

  5. Who played a deaf woman in *And Now Tomorrow*?

  6. Who was Oscar-nominated for the tearjerker *The Blue Veil*?

  7. Who played a blonde moll reformed by prison in *Because of You*?

  8. Who starred with James Stewart in the comedy *Magic Town*?

  9. Who made five films with David Niven?

  10. Who played the female lead in a Billy Wilder Best Picture Oscar winner?

62. Ava Gardner or Lana Turner?

  1. Who starred with Clark Gable four times?

  2. Who starred in Joseph L. Mankiewicz's 1954 film about Hollywood?

  3. Who starred in Vincente Minnelli's 1952 film about Hollywood?

  4. Who starred in the 1955 remake of *The Rains Came*?

  5. Who took Joan Crawford's role in a remake of *Grand Hotel*?

  6. Who appeared briefly as a model in *Two Girls and a Sailor*?

  7. Who was the first to receive a Best Actress Oscar nomination?

  8. Who appeared with Mickey Rooney in *Love Finds Andy Hardy*?

  9. Who was in *Ghosts on the Loose* with Bela Lugosi and The East Side Kids?

  10. Who took Mary Martin's role in the film version of a 1943 Broadway musical?

63.   Audrey Hepburn or Grace Kelly?

1. Who won an Oscar for playing a princess?
2. Who acted with Peter Finch in a Fred Zinnemann drama?
3. Who took Wendy Hiller's role in a remake of a Shaw comedy?
4. Who took Mary Astor's role in a remake of a sexy 1932 hit?
5. Who was paired with Gary Cooper in a Billy Wilder comedy?
6. Who starred with Stewart Granger in *Green Fire*?
7. Who sang an Oscar-nominated song in a 1956 MGM musical?
8. Who was Oscar-nominated in the Best Supporting Actress category?
9. Who was directed by William Wyler three times?
10. Who fell for Louis Jourdan in a 1956 romantic comedy?

Six
The Player

64. Match the actress to the film in which she played a secretary.

1. Ellen Corby
2. Lucille Ball
3. Eve Arden
4. Lee Patrick
5. Jean Hagen
6. Nina Foch
7. Thelma Ritter
8. June Havoc
9. Jean Harlow
10. Edie Adams

a. *Anatomy of a Murder*
b. *Gentleman's Agreement*
c. *The Dark Corner*
d. *Sunrise at Campobello*
e. *The Apartment*
f. *Sabrina* (1954)
g. *Executive Suite*
h. *Wife vs. Secretary*
i. *The Maltese Falcon* (1941)
j. *Daddy Long Legs* (1955)

65. Match the actor to the film in which he played an Asian character (not always convincingly).

1. Walter Huston   a. *A Majority of One*
2. Ricardo Montalban   b. *Breakfast at Tiffany's*
3. Orson Welles   c. *The Hatchet Man*
4. Alec Guinness   d. *Dragon Seed*
5. Paul Muni   e. *The Left Hand of God*
6. Edward G. Robinson   f. *Sayonara*
7. Lee J. Cobb   g. *The Inn of the Sixth Happiness*
8. Mickey Rooney   h. *The Black Rose*
9. Marlon Brando   i. *The Good Earth*
10. Robert Donat   j. *The Teahouse of the August Moon*

66. Match the "bad girl" to the film in which she was "bad."

1. Gloria Grahame   a. *The Killing*
2. Peggy Cummins   b. *Nightmare Alley*
3. Jan Sterling   c. *Sudden Fear*
4. Helen Walker   d. *Criss Cross*
5. Marie Windsor   e. *Dead Reckoning*
6. Marilyn Maxwell   f. *Female on the Beach*
7. Lizabeth Scott   g. *Out of the Past*
8. Audrey Totter   h. *Gun Crazy*
9. Jane Greer   i. *Champion*
10. Yvonne De Carlo   j. *Tension*

67. Match the actor to the film in which he played the man on the case (cop, detective, inspector…you get the idea).

1. Glenn Ford   **a.** *Shadow of a Doubt*
2. Cornel Wilde   **b.** *Dial M for Murder*
3. Macdonald Carey   **c.** *Murder, My Sweet*
4. George Raft   **d.** *Cry of the City*
5. Barry Fitzgerald   **e.** *The Big Combo*
6. Ralph Meeker   **f.** *I Confess*
7. Karl Malden   **g.** *The Naked City*
8. John Williams   **h.** *Kiss Me Deadly*
9. Dick Powell   **i.** *Black Widow* (1954)
10. Victor Mature   **j.** *The Big Heat*

68. Match the actress to the film in which she played a nun. No, Joan Collins is not a typo.

1. Joan Collins   **a.** *Green Dolphin Street*
2. Peggy Wood   **b.** *Black Narcissus*
3. Edith Evans   **c.** *Come to the Stable*
4. Rosalind Russell   **d.** *Portrait of Jennie*
5. Gladys Cooper   **e.** *The Singing Nun*
6. Celeste Holm   **f.** *The Trouble with Angels*
7. Lillian Gish   **g.** *The Nun's Story*
8. Deborah Kerr   **h.** *The Sound of Music*
9. Greer Garson   **i.** *The Song of Bernadette*
10. Donna Reed   **j.** *Sea Wife*

69.   Match the actor to the film in which he played a character with what were once referred to as "homosexual tendencies."

1. Martin Landau   **a.** *Billy Budd*
2. Robert Ryan   **b.** *The Sergeant*
3. Don Murray   **c.** *Rope*
4. Farley Granger   **d.** *Inside Daisy Clover*
5. Wendell Corey   **e.** *Victim*
6. Dirk Bogarde   **f.** *North by Northwest*
7. Rod Steiger   **g.** *Ben-Hur* (1959)
8. Robert Redford   **h.** *Advise and Consent*
9. Anthony Hopkins   **i.** *The Lion in Winter*
10. Stephen Boyd   **j.** *Desert Fury*

70.   Match the nonblond actress to the film for which she became a blonde.

1. Anne Baxter   **a.** *Forever Amber*
2. Natalie Wood   **b.** *The Silver Chalice*
3. Gene Tierney   **c.** *The Fuzzy Pink Nightgown*
4. Jane Russell   **d.** *Beat the Devil*
5. Linda Darnell   **e.** *The Diary of a Chambermaid* (1946)
6. Mary Astor   **f.** *I Confess*
7. Shirley MacLaine   **g.** *The Palm Beach Story*
8. Jennifer Jones   **h.** *The Lady from Shanghai*
9. Rita Hayworth   **i.** *A Bell for Adano*
10. Paulette Goddard   **j.** *Career*

71. Match the "angry young man" of the British film world to the film
     in which he starred (and vented his frustrations).

1. Richard Burton	**a.** *This Sporting Life*	
2. Laurence Harvey	**b.** *Saturday Night and Sunday Morning*	
3. David Warner	**c.** *If...*	
4. Alan Bates	**d.** *Morgan!*	
5. Tom Courtenay	**e.** *Room at the Top*	
6. Richard Harris	**f.** *The L-Shaped Room*	
7. Tom Bell	**g.** *A Kind of Loving*	
8. Albert Finney	**h.** *Look Back in Anger*	
9. Malcolm McDowell	**i.** *The Angry Silence*	
10. Richard Attenborough	**j.** *The Loneliness of the Long Distance Runner*	

72. Match the actress to the western in which she appeared.

1. Virginia Mayo	**a.** *The Naked Spur*
2. Janet Leigh	**b.** *Gunfight at the O.K. Corral*
3. Carroll Baker	**c.** *Pursued*
4. Ann Sheridan	**d.** *Colorado Territory*
5. Susan Hayward	**e.** *Winchester '73*
6. Teresa Wright	**f.** *Dodge City*
7. Jean Arthur	**g.** *Man Without a Star*
8. Shelley Winters	**h.** *Rawhide*
9. Rhonda Fleming	**i.** *The Big Country*
10. Jeanne Crain	**j.** *Arizona*

73. Match the performer to the film in which he/she was blind.

1. Claude Rains	a. *The Enchanted Cottage*
2. Ida Lupino	b. *Thunder in the East*
3. Dana Andrews	c. *Night Song*
4. James Cagney	d. *Pride of the Marines*
5. Herbert Marshall	e. *Mr. Skeffington*
6. John Garfield	f. *The Light That Failed*
7. Van Johnson	g. *Bright Victory*
8. Ronald Colman	h. *On Dangerous Ground*
9. Deborah Kerr	i. *23 Paces to Baker Street*
10. Arthur Kennedy	j. *City for Conquest*

74. In the years of the studio system, actresses played women with a surprising range of careers that went far beyond wives and mothers. Match the actress to her profession.

1. Jean Arthur in *A Foreign Affair*	a. congresswoman
2. Claudette Colbert in *Private Worlds*	b. general physician
3. Katharine Hepburn in *Christopher Strong*	c. engineering teacher and lecturer
4. Bette Davis in *Ex-Lady*	d. aviatrix
5. Myrna Loy in *Belles on Their Toes*	e. concert pianist
6. Mary Astor in *The Great Lie*	f. newspaper columnist
7. Greer Garson in *Blossoms in the Dust*	g. restaurant chain owner
8. Barbara Stanwyck in *Meet John Doe*	h. psychiatrist
9. Joan Crawford in *Mildred Pierce*	i. commercial artist
10. Jennifer Jones in *Love Is a Many-Splendored Thing*	j. children's rights activist

75. Match the performer to the film in which he/she had amnesia.

1.	Greta Garbo	a.	*Random Harvest*
2.	Boris Karloff	b.	*I Love You Again*
3.	Ingrid Bergman	c.	*Singapore*
4.	William Powell	d.	*Spellbound*
5.	Jennifer Jones	e.	*Libel*
6.	John Hodiak	f.	*Charlie Chan at the Opera*
7.	Ava Gardner	g.	*Love Letters*
8.	Ronald Colman	h.	*Anastasia*
9.	Dirk Bogarde	i.	*As You Desire Me*
10.	Gregory Peck	j.	*Somewhere in the Night*

76. Sagas of unwed mothers were a staple of what were once known as "women's pictures." Match the actress to the film in which she got pregnant without being married (or had done so in her past).

1.	Katharine Hepburn	a.	*To Each His Own*
2.	Margaret Sullavan	b.	*A Woman Rebels*
3.	Bette Davis	c.	*The Sin of Madelon Claudet*
4.	Olivia de Havilland	d.	*My Foolish Heart*
5.	Joan Fontaine	e.	*Only Yesterday*
6.	Helen Hayes	f.	*The Life of Vergie Winters*
7.	Lana Turner	g.	*The Old Maid*
8.	Susan Hayward	h.	*White Banners*
9.	Fay Bainter	i.	*Letter from an Unknown Woman*
10.	Ann Harding	j.	*Peyton Place*

77. Match the comedy star to the feature film in which he/she starred.

1. Buster Keaton   **a.** *The Patsy*
2. Charlie Chaplin   **b.** *The Party*
3. Harold Lloyd   **c.** *The Navigator*
4. W.C. Fields   **d.** *The Freshman*
5. Mae West   **e.** *The Circus*
6. Groucho Marx   **f.** *A Southern Yankee*
7. Danny Kaye   **g.** *It's a Gift*
8. Red Skelton   **h.** *Go West, Young Man*
9. Jerry Lewis   **i.** *Up in Arms*
10. Peter Sellers   **j.** *Copacabana*

78. Vivien Leigh's Scarlett O'Hara will forever be the "Southern belle" performance by which all others are measured. Match each actress to the film in which she did her own version of a flirtatious and/or headstrong magnolia blossom.

1. Patricia Neal   **a.** *Jezebel*
2. Susan Hayward   **b.** *Wells Fargo*
3. Margaret Sullavan   **c.** *Tap Roots*
4. Bette Davis   **d.** *Belle Starr*
5. Arlene Dahl   **e.** *So Red the Rose*
6. Gene Tierney   **f.** *Another Part of the Forest*
7. Elizabeth Taylor   **g.** *Bright Leaf*
8. Frances Dee   **h.** *Raintree County*
9. Constance Towers   **i.** *A Southern Yankee*
10. Ann Blyth   **j.** *The Horse Soldiers*

79. Match the performer to the film in which he/she played two roles (anything from twins to inexplicable lookalikes). I apologize for excluding Maria Montez's unforgettable work in *Cobra Woman*.

1. Douglas Fairbanks, Jr.   a. *The Prisoner of Zenda* (1937)
2. Sylvia Sidney   b. *Here Come the Waves*
3. Edward G. Robinson   c. *That Night in Rio*
4. Betty Hutton   d. *The Whole Town's Talking*
5. Danny Kaye   e. *The Black Room*
6. Olivia de Havilland   f. *A Stolen Life*
7. Boris Karloff   g. *The Corsican Brothers*
8. Ronald Colman   h. *On the Riviera*
9. Bette Davis   i. *Thirty-Day Princess*
10. Don Ameche   j. *The Dark Mirror*

Seven

The Winning Team

80.   Match the director to the actress he married.

1. William Wyler	a. Merle Oberon
2. Anatole Litvak	b. Veronica Lake
3. Alexander Korda	c. Rita Hayworth
4. Orson Welles	d. Ann Todd
5. John Huston	e. Margaret Sullavan
6. Andre de Toth	f. Gloria Grahame
7. Richard Brooks	g. Evelyn Keyes
8. David Lean	h. Miriam Hopkins
9. Nicholas Ray	i. Maureen O'Sullivan
10. John Farrow	j. Jean Simmons

81.   Match the movie stars who were married to each other.

1. Lew Ayres	a. Madeleine Carroll
2. John Payne	b. Paulette Goddard
3. William Powell	c. Ginger Rogers
4. Sterling Hayden	d. Rita Hayworth
5. Mickey Rooney	e. Ida Lupino
6. Dick Haymes	f. Eleanor Powell
7. Glenn Ford	g. Gloria DeHaven
8. Louis Hayward	h. Alice Faye
9. Burgess Meredith	i. Carole Lombard
10. Tony Martin	j. Ava Gardner

82.   Match the married couple to the film in which they appeared together (before or during the marriage).

1. Jean Simmons/ Stewart Granger	a. *This Is My Affair*
2. Anne Baxter/ John Hodiak	b. *Woman in Hiding*
3. Joan Crawford/ Franchot Tone	c. *Sunday Dinner for a Soldier*
4. Frances Dee/ Joel McCrea	d. *The Bride Wore Red*
5. Jessica Tandy/ Hume Cronyn	e. *Another Part of the Forest*
6. Florence Eldridge/ Fredric March	f. *The Green Years*
7. Barbara Stanwyck/ Robert Taylor	g. *Footsteps in the Fog*
8. Ida Lupino/ Howard Duff	h. *Brother Rat*
9. June Allyson/ Dick Powell	i. *The Silver Cord*
10. Jane Wyman/ Ronald Reagan	j. *The Reformer and the Redhead*

83.   Match the screen team to one of their lesser-known movies.

1. Myrna Loy/ William Powell
2. Greer Garson/ Walter Pidgeon
3. Dorothy Lamour/ Bob Hope
4. June Allyson/ Van Johnson
5. Judy Garland/ Mickey Rooney
6. Lauren Bacall/ Humphrey Bogart
7. Virginia Mayo/ Danny Kaye
8. Veronica Lake/ Alan Ladd
9. Jean Harlow/ Clark Gable
10. Bud Abbott/ Lou Costello

a. *Remains to Be Seen*
b. *Hold Your Man*
c. *Double Wedding*
d. *Scandal at Scourie*
e. *Here Come the Co-Eds*
f. *The Kid from Brooklyn*
g. *Thoroughbreds Don't Cry*
h. *Saigon*
i. *Dark Passage*
j. *Caught in the Draft*

84.   Match the screen team to the musical in which they co-starred.

1. Kathryn Grayson/ Mario Lanza
2. Kathryn Grayson/ Howard Keel
3. Ruby Keeler/ Dick Powell
4. Jane Powell/ Vic Damone
5. Vera-Ellen/ Fred Astaire
6. Betty Grable/ Dan Dailey
7. Esther Williams/ Van Johnson
8. Ginger Rogers/ Fred Astaire
9. Esther Williams/ Howard Keel
10. Jeanette MacDonald/ Maurice Chevalier

a. *Call Me Mister*
b. *One Hour With You*
c. *Shipmates Forever*
d. *Jupiter's Darling*
e. *Lovely to Look At*
f. *Thrill of a Romance*
g. *Rich, Young and Pretty*
h. *That Midnight Kiss*
i. *The Belle of New York*
j. *Carefree*

85.   Match the actor and actress who appeared together in three films.

1. David Niven	**a.** Ava Gardner
2. Jack Lemmon	**b.** Ginger Rogers
3. Cary Grant	**c.** June Allyson
4. Leslie Howard	**d.** Ingrid Bergman
5. Charles Boyer	**e.** Myrna Loy
6. James Stewart	**f.** Jean Simmons
7. James Mason	**g.** Bette Davis
8. Tyrone Power	**h.** Anne Baxter
9. Charles Laughton	**i.** Kim Novak
10. Robert Mitchum	**j.** Maureen O'Hara

86.   Match the screen team to the number of films they made together.

1. Doris Day/ Rock Hudson	**a.** 1
2. Katharine Hepburn/ Spencer Tracy	**b.** 2
3. Maria Montez/ Jon Hall	**c.** 3
4. Grace Kelly/ Cary Grant	**d.** 4
5. Joan Crawford/ Clark Gable	**e.** 5
6. Margaret Sullavan/ James Stewart	**f.** 6
7. Claudette Colbert/ Fred MacMurray	**g.** 7
8. Shirley MacLaine/ Jack Lemmon	**h.** 8
9. Loretta Young/ Tyrone Power	**i.** 9
10. Ginger Rogers/ Fred Astaire	**j.** 10

87.   Match the co-stars of a famous film to the less-remembered film in which they had previously appeared together.

1. Merle Oberon and Laurence Olivier in *Wuthering Heights*

    a. *The Divorce of Lady X*

2. Carole Lombard and Fredric March in *Nothing Sacred*

    b. *A Yank at Oxford*

3. Marilyn Monroe and David Wayne in *How to Marry a Millionaire*

    c. *Me and My Gal*

4. Kathryn Grayson and Gene Kelly in *Anchors Aweigh*

    d. *Trouble for Two*

5. Joan Bennett and Spencer Tracy in *Father of the Bride*

    e. *Sylvia Scarlett*

6. Olivia de Havilland and Leslie Howard in *Gone With the Wind*

    f. *Thousands Cheer*

7. Vivien Leigh and Robert Taylor in *Waterloo Bridge*

    g. *The Secret Six*

8. Rosalind Russell and Robert Montgomery in *Night Must Fall*

    h. *We're Not Married*

9. Jean Harlow and Wallace Beery in *Dinner at Eight*

    i. *It's Love I'm After*

10. Katharine Hepburn and Cary Grant in *Bringing Up Baby*

    j. *The Eagle and the Hawk*

88. Who was **not** one of these titular threesomes?

1. *A Letter to Three Wives*
   a. Ann Sothern; b. Linda Darnell; c. Dorothy McGuire; d. Jeanne Crain

2. *Three Comrades*
   a. Walter Pidgeon; b. Franchot Tone; c. Robert Taylor; d. Robert Young

3. *These Three*
   a. Miriam Hopkins; b. Fredric March; c. Merle Oberon; d. Joel McCrea

4. *Three on a Match*
   a. Bette Davis; b. Ann Dvorak; c. Constance Bennett; d. Joan Blondell

5. *The Three Musketeers* (1948)
   a. Peter Lawford; b. Robert Coote; c. Gig Young; d. Van Heflin

6. *Three Little Girls in Blue*
   a. Vera-Ellen; b. Joan Caulfield; c. Vivian Blaine; d. June Haver

7. *Three Strangers*
   a. Peter Lorre; b. Sydney Greenstreet; c. Claude Rains; d. Geraldine Fitzgerald

8. *Three Guys Named Mike*
   a. Van Johnson; b. Howard Keel; c. Barry Sullivan; d. John Hodiak

9. *Three Godfathers*
   a. Victor McLaglen; b. John Wayne; c. Harry Carey, Jr.; d. Pedro Armendariz

10. *Tom, Dick and Harry*
    a. Alan Marshal; b. George Murphy; c. Burgess Meredith; d. Dennis Morgan

Eight

A Song to Remember

89. Match the musical performer to the film in which he/she sang a song or two (before or after becoming famous).

1. Nelson Eddy	**a.** *Pete Kelly's Blues*
2. Jeanette MacDonald	**b.** *The Gay Divorcee*
3. Howard Keel	**c.** *Girl Crazy* (1943)
4. Ella Fitzgerald	**d.** *Follow the Boys*
5. June Allyson	**e.** *Deep in My Heart*
6. Julie London	**f.** *Panama Hattie*
7. Louis Armstrong	**g.** *Dancing Lady*
8. Lena Horne	**h.** *Sun Valley Serenade*
9. Betty Grable	**i.** *High Society*
10. Dorothy Dandridge	**j.** *The Girl Can't Help It*

90. Match the song standard to the film that introduced it.

1. "I've Got My Love to Keep Me Warm"   **a.** *Babes on Broadway*

2. "Isn't It Romantic?"   **b.** *Follow the Fleet*

3. "Long Ago and Far Away"   **c.** *Love Me Tonight*

4. "How About You?"   **d.** *Dames*

5. "I've Got You Under My Skin"   **e.** *A Damsel in Distress*

6. "Let's Face the Music and Dance"   **f.** *Gold Diggers of 1933*

7. "They Can't Take That Away from Me"   **g.** *On the Avenue*

8. "A Foggy Day"   **h.** *Cover Girl*

9. "I Only Have Eyes for You"   **i.** *Shall We Dance*

10. "We're in the Money"   **j.** *Born to Dance*

91. Match the song to the film for which it won an Oscar for Best Song.

1. "You'll Never Know"   **a.** *Hello, Frisco, Hello*

2. "The Continental"   **b.** *Lady Be Good*

3. "Mona Lisa"   **c.** *A Hole in the Head*

4. "Buttons and Bows"   **d.** *Going My Way*

5. "The Last Time I Saw Paris"   **e.** *Swing Time*

6. "Thanks for the Memory"   **f.** *The Gay Divorcee*

7. "The Way You Look Tonight"   **g.** *The Paleface*

8. "Swinging on a Star"   **h.** *Here Comes the Groom*

9. "High Hopes"   **i.** *Captain Carey, U.S.A.*

10. "In the Cool, Cool, Cool of the Evening"   **j.** *The Big Broadcast of 1938*

92. Match the singer to the film in which he/she provided the singing voice for the title tune or theme song.

1. Peggy Lee	**a.** *Friendly Persuasion*
2. Johnny Mathis	**b.** *High Noon*
3. Vic Damone	**c.** *Three Coins in the Fountain*
4. Pat Boone	**d.** *Johnny Guitar*
5. Nat "King" Cole	**e.** *Return to Peyton Place*
6. Tex Ritter	**f.** *The Best of Everything*
7. Rosemary Clooney	**g.** *Love with the Proper Stranger*
8. Frank Sinatra	**h.** *An Affair to Remember*
9. Jack Jones	**i.** *Thunderball*
10. Tom Jones	**j.** *Raintree County*

93. Match the screen adaptation of a Broadway musical to the song that was added to its score for the film version.

1. *Roberta*	**a.** "Anyone Here for Love?"
2. *Good News* (1947)	**b.** "Something Good"
3. *Gentlemen Prefer Blondes*	**c.** "Lovely to Look At"
4. *Guys and Dolls*	**d.** "Fated to Be Mated"
5. *On the Town*	**e.** "A Woman in Love"
6. *Damn Yankees*	**f.** "There's Something About an Empty Chair"
7. *The Sound of Music*	**g.** "Pass That Peace Pipe"
8. *Silk Stockings*	**h.** "You're Awful"
9. *South Pacific*	**i.** "I Have the Room Above Her"
10. *Show Boat* (1936)	**j.** "My Girl Back Home"

94. Match the Broadway composer to the film for which he wrote the music for original songs.

1. Jerome Kern   a. *Seven Brides for Seven Brothers*
2. Cole Porter   b. *Anchors Aweigh*
3. Gene de Paul   c. *Gigi*
4. Frank Loesser   d. *Centennial Summer*
5. Frederick Loewe   e. *A Damsel in Distress*
6. Jule Styne   f. *On the Avenue*
7. George Gershwin   g. *The Pirate*
8. Irving Berlin   h. *Hallelujah, I'm a Bum*
9. Richard Rodgers   i. *Hans Christian Andersen*
10. Kurt Weill   j. *Where Do We Go from Here?*

95. Match the song to the film in which it is sung by Marlene Dietrich.

1. "Falling in Love Again"   a. *Desire*
2. "You've Got That Look That   b. *Seven Sinners*
   Leaves Me Weak"
3. "What Am I Bid for My   c. *A Foreign Affair*
   Apples?"
4. "I Can't Give You Anything   d. *Blonde Venus*
   But Love"
5. "Hot Voodoo"   e. *Stage Fright*
6. "The Laziest Gal in Town"   f. *Destry Rides Again*
7. "Awake in a Dream"   g. *The Flame of New
                                     Orleans*
8. "Sweet Is the Blush of May"   h. *The Blue Angel*
9. "Get Away Young Man"   i. *Rancho Notorious*
10. "Black Market"   j. *Morocco*

96.   Match the song to the film in which it is sung by Frank Sinatra.

1. "All My Tomorrows"

2. "The Lady Is a Tramp"

3. "All the Way"

4. "I Fall in Love Too Easily"

5. "Time After Time"

6. "Sue Me"

7. "You're Sensational"

8. "Just One of Those Things"

9. "My Kind of Town"

10. "I Couldn't Sleep a Wink Last Night"

a. *Anchors Aweigh*

b. *A Hole in the Head*

c. *Young at Heart*

d. *Guys and Dolls*

e. *Pal Joey*

f. *Higher and Higher*

g. *It Happened in Brooklyn*

h. *Robin and the Seven Hoods*

i. *The Joker Is Wild*

j. *High Society*

97. Match the song to the usually non-singing performers who sing it (in an informal setting) in a movie.

1. "Night and Day"

2. "Over the Rainbow"

3. "Swanee River"

4. "After You've Gone"

5. "I Can't Give You Anything But Love"

6. "Yes! We Have No Bananas"

7. "Buffalo Gals"

8. "Who's Afraid of the Big Bad Wolf?"

9. "Shuffle Off to Buffalo"

10. "Let's Fall in Love"

a. Audrey Hepburn in *Sabrina*

b. Jack Lemmon and Judy Holliday in *It Should Happen to You*

c. Katharine Hepburn in *Desk Set*

d. James Stewart and Donna Reed in *It's a Wonderful Life*

e. James Stewart in *The Philadelphia Story*

f. Bette Davis in *Dead Ringer*

g. Clark Gable in *It Happened One Night*

h. Shirley MacLaine in *Some Came Running*

i. Jean Arthur in *Mr. Deeds Goes to Town*

j. Cary Grant and Katharine Hepburn in *Bringing Up Baby*

Nine

Boy Meets Girl

98. Match the actress to the film in which she appeared with James Cagney.

1. Jean Harlow
2. Rita Hayworth
3. Sylvia Sidney
4. Gladys George
5. Ann Sheridan
6. Virginia Mayo
7. Dorothy Malone
8. Bette Davis
9. Gloria Stuart
10. Barbara Stanwyck

a. *The Roaring Twenties*
b. *These Wilder Years*
c. *The Public Enemy*
d. *White Heat*
e. *Man of a Thousand Faces*
f. *The Strawberry Blonde*
g. *Jimmy the Gent*
h. *Angels with Dirty Faces*
i. *Blood on the Sun*
j. *Here Comes the Navy*

99. Match the actor to the film in which he appeared with Myrna Loy.

1. Montgomery Clift   a. *Too Hot to Handle*
2. Clark Gable   b. *The Rains Came*
3. John Barrymore   c. *Broadway Bill*
4. Warner Baxter   d. *Love Crazy*
5. Paul Newman   e. *Lonelyhearts*
6. Ronald Colman   f. *From the Terrace*
7. Tyrone Power   g. *Love Me Tonight*
8. William Powell   h. *Topaze*
9. Maurice Chevalier   i. *Arrowsmith*
10. Leslie Howard   j. *The Animal Kingdom*

100. Match the actress to the film in which she appeared with Henry Fonda.

1. Ginger Rogers   a. *Drums Along the Mohawk*
2. Barbara Stanwyck   b. *That Certain Woman*
3. Margaret Sullavan   c. *The Farmer Takes a Wife*
4. Linda Darnell   d. *Tales of Manhattan*
5. Sylvia Sidney   e. *Chad Hanna*
6. Janet Gaynor   f. *The Male Animal*
7. Bette Davis   g. *The Mad Miss Manton*
8. Claudette Colbert   h. *The Big Street*
9. Olivia de Havilland   i. *The Moon's Our Home*
10. Lucille Ball   j. *You Only Live Once*

101.   Match the actor to the film in which he appeared with Ginger Rogers.

1. James Stewart	**a.** *Having Wonderful Time*
2. Joel McCrea	**b.** *It Had to Be You*
3. Ray Milland	**c.** *Primrose Path*
4. Cary Grant	**d.** *Week-End at the Waldorf*
5. Walter Pidgeon	**e.** *Once Upon A Honeymoon*
6. Ronald Colman	**f.** *Tight Spot*
7. Douglas Fairbanks, Jr.	**g.** *Vivacious Lady*
8. Clifton Webb	**h.** *Lucky Partners*
9. Cornel Wilde	**i.** *The Major and the Minor*
10. Edward G. Robinson	**j.** *Dreamboat*

102.   Match the actress to the film in which she appeared with Bob Hope.

1. Katharine Hepburn	**a.** *My Favorite Spy*
2. Lucille Ball	**b.** *My Favorite Blonde*
3. Madeleine Carroll	**c.** *My Favorite Brunette*
4. Eva Marie Saint	**d.** *That Certain Feeling*
5. Arlene Dahl	**e.** *The Iron Petticoat*
6. Dorothy Lamour	**f.** *Fancy Pants*
7. Rhonda Fleming	**g.** *Nothing But the Truth*
8. Hedy Lamarr	**h.** *Let's Face It*
9. Paulette Goddard	**i.** *The Great Lover*
10. Betty Hutton	**j.** *Here Come the Girls*

103.   Match the actor to the film in which he appeared with Ingrid Bergman.

1. Jose Ferrer	**a.** *Anastasia*
2. Gary Cooper	**b.** *Joan of Arc*
3. Cary Grant	**c.** *Rage in Heaven*
4. Robert Montgomery	**d.** *The Inn of the Sixth Happiness*
5. Anthony Perkins	**e.** *Arch of Triumph*
6. Yul Brynner	**f.** *The Yellow Rolls-Royce*
7. Charles Boyer	**g.** *Indiscreet*
8. Joseph Cotten	**h.** *Goodbye Again*
9. Omar Sharif	**i.** *Saratoga Trunk*
10. Curt Jurgens	**j.** *Under Capricorn*

104.   Match the actress to the film in which she appeared with William Holden.

1. Grace Kelly	**a.** *Escape from Fort Bravo*
2. Deborah Kerr	**b.** *Forever Female*
3. Jeanne Crain	**c.** *The Counterfeit Traitor*
4. Veronica Lake	**d.** *The Bridges at Toko-Ri*
5. Lilli Palmer	**e.** *The Proud and the Profane*
6. Loretta Young	**f.** *The Key*
7. Lucille Ball	**g.** *Apartment for Peggy*
8. Sophia Loren	**h.** *Rachel and the Stranger*
9. Ginger Rogers	**i.** *I Wanted Wings*
10. Eleanor Parker	**j.** *Miss Grant Takes Richmond*

105. Match the actor to the film in which he appeared with Betty Grable.

1. Victor Mature	**a.** *How to Marry a Millionaire*
2. Tyrone Power	**b.** *Three for the Show*
3. Jack Lemmon	**c.** *How to Be Very, Very Popular*
4. Rory Calhoun	**d.** *Mother Wore Tights*
5. Douglas Fairbanks, Jr.	**e.** *A Yank in the R.A.F.*
6. Dan Dailey	**f.** *Billy Rose's Diamond Horseshoe*
7. Robert Young	**g.** *The Dolly Sisters*
8. Robert Cummings	**h.** *Wabash Avenue*
9. John Payne	**i.** *That Lady in Ermine*
10. Dick Haymes	**j.** *Sweet Rosie O'Grady*

106. Match the actress to the film in which she appeared with Gregory Peck.

1. Greer Garson	**a.** *The Great Sinner*
2. Joan Bennett	**b.** *Yellow Sky*
3. Sophia Loren	**c.** *The Macomber Affair*
4. Deborah Kerr	**d.** *Captain Horatio Hornblower*
5. Jean Simmons	**e.** *The Valley of Decision*
6. Ava Gardner	**f.** *The Big Country*
7. Virginia Mayo	**g.** *Designing Woman*
8. Jennifer Jones	**h.** *Beloved Infidel*
9. Anne Baxter	**i.** *Arabesque*
10. Lauren Bacall	**j.** *The Man in the Gray Flannel Suit*

107.   Match the actor to the film in which he appeared with Doris Day.

1. James Cagney	**a**. *Please Don't Eat the Daisies*
2. Louis Jourdan	**b**. *The Winning Team*
3. David Niven	**c**. *Teacher's Pet*
4. Rex Harrison	**d**. *The West Point Story*
5. Clark Gable	**e**. *I'll See You in My Dreams*
6. Richard Widmark	**f**. *The Tunnel of Love*
7. Jack Lemmon	**g**. *Julie*
8. Danny Thomas	**h**. *Lover Come Back*
9. Ronald Reagan	**i**. *It Happened to Jane*
10. Rock Hudson	**j**. *Midnight Lace*

Ten

Golden Boy

108. Match the film to the Academy Award it received.

1. *Citizen Kane*	**a.** 1937 Best Actress
2. *The Great Ziegfeld*	**b.** 1936 Best Director
3. *The Good Earth*	**c.** 1937 Best Actor
4. *Rebecca*	**d.** 1940 Best Director
5. *Captains Courageous*	**e.** 1936 Best Picture
6. *The Grapes of Wrath*	**f.** 1941 Best Picture
7. *The Awful Truth*	**g.** 1937 Best Picture
8. *The Life of Emile Zola*	**h.** 1941 Best Original Screenplay
9. *How Green Was My Valley*	**i.** 1937 Best Director
10. *Mr. Deeds Goes to Town*	**j.** 1940 Best Picture

109.   The following stars won many Oscar nominations. For each, pick the one performance that was **not** nominated.

1. Greer Garson
a. *Goodbye, Mr. Chips*; **b.** *Pride and Prejudice*; **c.** *Blossoms in the Dust*; **d.** *Madame Curie*

2. Paul Newman
a. *Hud*; **b.** *The Hustler*; **c.** *Somebody Up There Likes Me*; **d.** *Cool Hand Luke*

3. Richard Burton
a. *The Robe*; **b.** *The Night of the Iguana*; **c.** *The Spy Who Came in from the Cold*; **d.** *My Cousin Rachel*

4. Greta Garbo
a. *Anna Christie*; **b.** *Romance*; **c.** *Grand Hotel*; **d.** *Ninotchka*

5. Bette Davis
a. *Of Human Bondage*; **b.** *The Star*; **c.** *The Letter*; **d.** *Mr. Skeffington*

6. Paul Muni
a. *Scarface*; **b.** *The Last Angry Man*; **c.** *The Life of Emile Zola*; **d.** *The Story of Louis Pasteur*

7. Shirley MacLaine
a. *Some Came Running*; **b.** *Irma La Douce*; **c.** *The Apartment*; **d.** *The Children's Hour*

8. Elizabeth Taylor
a. *Cat on a Hot Tin Roof*; **b.** *Raintree County*; **c.** *Suddenly, Last Summer*; **d.** *Giant*

9. Katharine Hepburn
a. *Woman of the Year*; **b.** *Little Women*; **c.** *The Rainmaker*; **d.** *Suddenly, Last Summer*

10. Mickey Rooney
a. *National Velvet*; **b.** *Babes in Arms*; **c.** *The Human Comedy*; **d.** *The Bold and the Brave*

110.   Pick the film for which each man won a Best Director Oscar.

1. Vincente Minnelli   **a.** *Meet Me in St. Louis*; **b.** *Lust for Life*; **c.** *An American in Paris*; **d.** *Gigi*

2. George Cukor   **a.** *Camille*; **b.** *Dinner at Eight*; **c.** *Gaslight*; **d.** *My Fair Lady*

3. John Ford   **a.** *Stagecoach*; **b.** *My Darling Clementine*; **c.** *The Quiet Man*; **d.** *The Searchers*

4. Victor Fleming   **a.** *Gone With the Wind*; **b.** *The Wizard of Oz*; **c.** *Captains Courageous*; **d.** *Joan of Arc*

5. Michael Curtiz   **a.** *Angels with Dirty Faces*; **b.** *Casablanca*; **c.** *Yankee Doodle Dandy*; **d.** *Mildred Pierce*

6. George Stevens   **a.** *Gunga Din*; **b.** *Shane*; **c.** *The More the Merrier*; **d.** *Giant*

7. John Huston   **a.** *The Treasure of the Sierra Madre*; **b.** *Moby Dick*; **c.** *The Maltese Falcon*; **d.** *The African Queen*

8. Billy Wilder   **a.** *Double Indemnity*; **b.** *The Lost Weekend*; **c.** *Sunset Boulevard*; **d.** *Some Like It Hot*

9. Elia Kazan   **a.** *A Tree Grows in Brooklyn*; **b.** *East of Eden*; **c.** *On the Waterfront*; **d.** *A Streetcar Named Desire*

10. Carol Reed   **a.** *Oliver!*; **b.** *Odd Man Out*; **c.** *The Fallen Idol*; **d.** *The Third Man*

111.   Pick the film for which each performer won an Oscar for a supporting role.

   1. Gloria Grahame   **a.** *It's a Wonderful Life*; **b.** *In a Lonely Place*; **c.** *The Big Heat*; **d.** *The Bad and the Beautiful*

   2. Van Heflin   **a.** *Johnny Eager*; **b.** *Battle Cry*; **c.** *Shane*; **d.** *Airport*

   3. Teresa Wright   **a.** *The Pride of the Yankees*; **b.** *Mrs. Miniver*; **c.** *The Little Foxes*; **d.** *The Best Years of Our Lives*

   4. Karl Malden   **a.** *On the Waterfront*; **b.** *Fear Strikes Out*; **c.** *A Streetcar Named Desire*; **d.** *One-Eyed Jacks*

   5. Anne Baxter   **a.** *The Magnificent Ambersons*; **b.** *The Razor's Edge*; **c.** *All About Eve*; **d.** *The Ten Commandments*

   6. Edmond O'Brien   **a.** *The Barefoot Contessa*; **b.** *Julius Caesar*; **c.** *The Killers*; **d.** *Seven Days in May*

   7. Mary Astor   **a.** *Dodsworth*; **b.** *The Maltese Falcon*; **c.** *The Great Lie*; **d.** *Meet Me in St. Louis*

   8. Anne Revere   **a.** *The Song of Bernadette*; **b.** *Body and Soul*; **c.** *Gentleman's Agreement*; **d.** *National Velvet*

   9. Walter Huston   **a.** *And Then There Were None*; **b.** *Duel in the Sun*; **c.** *The Treasure of the Sierra Madre*; **d.** *Of Human Hearts*

   10. Ethel Barrymore   **a.** *None But the Lonely Heart*; **b.** *Pinky*; **c.** *The Farmer's Daughter*; **d.** *The Spiral Staircase*

112.   Pick the film for which each star received his/her only Oscar nomination for acting.

1. Lana Turner
    a. *Imitation of Life*; **b.** *Peyton Place*;
    c. *The Postman Always Rings Twice*;
    d. *The Bad and the Beautiful*

2. Ava Gardner
    a. *Mogambo*; **b.** *Show Boat*;
    c. *On the Beach*; **d.** *The Night of the Iguana*

3. Gene Kelly
    a. *Anchors Aweigh*; **b.** *On the Town*;
    c. *An American in Paris*; **d.** *Singin' in the Rain*

4. Anthony Perkins
    a. *Psycho*; **b.** *Desire Under the Elms*;
    c. *Fear Strikes Out*; **d.** *Friendly Persuasion*

5. Carole Lombard
    a. *Twentieth Century*; **b.** *Nothing Sacred*;
    c. *My Man Godfrey*; **d.** *To Be or Not to Be*

6. Tony Curtis
    a. *The Defiant Ones*; **b.** *Sweet Smell of Success*;
    c. *Some Like It Hot*; **d.** *The Boston Strangler*

7. Jean Arthur
    a. *Shane*; **b.** *The More the Merrier*;
    c. *Mr. Deeds Goes to Town*; **d.** *The Talk of the Town*

8. Robert Mitchum
    a. *Ryan's Daughter*; **b.** *The Sundowners*;
    c. *Story of G.I. Joe*; **d.** *Heaven Knows, Mr. Allison*

9. Orson Welles
    a. *Jane Eyre*; **b.** *The Stranger*;
    c. *Citizen Kane*; **d.** *Touch of Evil*

10. Dorothy McGuire
    a. *Friendly Persuasion*; **b.** *A Tree Grows in Brooklyn*;
    c. *The Spiral Staircase*; **d.** *Gentleman's Agreement*

113.   Match the actor to the year in which he received his only Oscar nomination for acting. Name the film as well. Also, name the only winner in the group (special Oscars don't count).

1. Fred Astaire		a. 1937
2. Robert Preston		b. 1940
3. Rock Hudson		c. 1945
4. Raymond Massey		d. 1950
5. Ralph Bellamy		e. 1956
6. Jeff Chandler		f. 1960
7. Cornel Wilde		g. 1966
8. John Mills		h. 1970
9. Trevor Howard		i. 1974
10. Steve McQueen		j. 1982

114.   Match the actress to the year in which she received her only Oscar nomination for acting. Name the film as well. Also, name the only winner in the group (special Oscars don't count).

1. Sylvia Sidney		a. 1930/31
2. Lee Remick		b. 1935
3. Lillian Gish		c. 1940
4. Joan Blondell		d. 1946
5. Peggy Ashcroft		e. 1951
6. Merle Oberon		f. 1956
7. Ann Sothern		g. 1962
8. Martha Scott		h. 1973
9. Marlene Dietrich		i. 1984
10. Carroll Baker		j. 1987

115.   Match the usually supporting player to the film for which he/she received a Best Actor/Best Actress Oscar nomination. Then name the only winner in the group.

1. Monty Woolley	a. *Wilson*
2. Gladys George	b. *The Front Page* (1931)
3. Adolphe Menjou	c. *Adventures of Robinson Crusoe*
4. May Robson	d. *The Pied Piper*
5. Louis Calhern	e. *Watch on the Rhine*
6. Edith Evans	f. *The Affairs of Cellini*
7. Alexander Knox	g. *The Whisperers*
8. Paul Lukas	h. *Lady for a Day*
9. Dan O'Herlihy	i. *Valiant Is the Word for Carrie*
10. Frank Morgan	j. *The Magnificent Yankee*

116.   Match the actress to the role that won her an Oscar. Then name the film.

1. Ingrid Bergman	a. Gloria Wandrous
2. Anne Bancroft	b. Lola Delaney
3. Grace Kelly	c. Paula Alquist
4. Katharine Hepburn	d. Ellie Andrews
5. Shirley Booth	e. Christina Drayton
6. Eva Marie Saint	f. Catherine Sloper
7. Elizabeth Taylor	g. Annie Sullivan
8. Claudette Colbert	h. Marylee Hadley
9. Olivia de Havilland	i. Edie Doyle
10. Dorothy Malone	j. Georgie Elgin

117. Match the Best Actor Academy Award performance to the actress who appeared with the actor in that film.

1. Gary Cooper in *Sergeant York*   **a.** Jane Wyman
2. Paul Scofield in *A Man for All Seasons*   **b.** Mala Powers
3. Charlton Heston in *Ben-Hur*   **c.** Lilia Skala
4. Ernest Borgnine in *Marty*   **d.** Wendy Hiller
5. Sidney Poitier in *Lilies of the Field*   **e.** Betsy Blair
6. Ray Milland in *The Lost Weekend*   **f.** Haya Harareet
7. Jose Ferrer in *Cyrano de Bergerac*   **g.** Joanne Dru
8. Laurence Olivier in *Hamlet*   **h.** Joan Bennett
9. George Arliss in *Disraeli*   **i.** Jean Simmons
10. Broderick Crawford in *All the King's Men*   **j.** Joan Leslie

118. Match the Best Actress Academy Award performance to the actor who appeared with the actress in that film.

1. Jane Wyman in *Johnny Belinda*   **a.** David Wayne
2. Joanne Woodward in *The Three Faces of Eve*   **b.** Franchot Tone
3. Judy Holliday in *Born Yesterday*   **c.** Charles Farrell
4. Janet Gaynor in *Seventh Heaven*   **d.** Jack Carson
5. Ginger Rogers in *Kitty Foyle*   **e.** Douglas Fairbanks, Jr.
6. Katharine Hepburn in *Morning Glory*   **f.** William Holden
7. Bette Davis in *Dangerous*   **g.** Chester Morris
8. Loretta Young in *The Farmer's Daughter*   **h.** Lew Ayres
9. Joan Crawford in *Mildred Pierce*   **i.** Dennis Morgan
10. Norma Shearer in *The Divorcee*   **j.** Joseph Cotten

119.   Match the star to the Oscar-related fact which describes him/her.

1. Joan Fontaine	**a.** Lost an Oscar to a sibling.
2. Walter Brennan	**b.** Got a Best Actress nomination for playing Jane Hudson.
3. Peter O'Toole	**c.** First performer to win an Oscar for a color film.
4. Audrey Hepburn	**d.** Nominated for a film directed by a spouse.
5. Olivia de Havilland	**e.** Only performer to win an Oscar for a Hitchcock film.
6. Raymond Massey	**f.** Nominated in 1954 for a role played on Broadway by Margaret Sullavan.
7. Arthur Kennedy	**g.** He and his son won nominations for playing real people.
8. Jean Simmons	**h.** Nominated for a musical remake of a film that won another performer an Oscar.
9. Richard Burton	**i.** Nominated for four films directed by the same man.
10. Katharine Hepburn	**j.** Nominated for a role that had previously won an Oscar for Charles Laughton.

Eleven

Once Is Not Enough

120. Match the Irene Dunne film to the actress who would reprise her role in a remake of that film. I hope Irene was flattered by the number of her films that were deemed remake-worthy (I didn't even include *Show Boat* and *Anna and the King of Siam*).

1. *Roberta*
2. *Love Affair*
3. *A Guy Named Joe*
4. *The Awful Truth*
5. *My Favorite Wife*
6. *Cimarron*
7. *Back Street*
8. *When Tomorrow Comes*
9. *The Age of Innocence*
10. *Magnificent Obsession*

a. Jane Wyman (with Ray Milland)
b. Jane Wyman (with Rock Hudson)
c. Doris Day
d. Kathryn Grayson
e. Deborah Kerr
f. Michelle Pfeiffer
g. June Allyson
h. Maria Schell
i. Margaret Sullavan
j. Holly Hunter

121. Match the MGM performance on the left to its MGM remake on the right.

1. Jean Harlow in *Red Dust*

   a. Judy Garland in *In the Good Old Summertime*

2. Norma Shearer in *The Women*

   b. Leslie Caron in *Gaby*

3. Greta Garbo in *Grand Hotel*

   c. Ava Gardner in *Mogambo*

4. Margaret Sullavan in *The Shop Around the Corner*

   d. Grace Kelly in *High Society*

5. Jean Harlow in *Libeled Lady*

   e. Lucille Ball in *Easy to Wed*

6. Greta Garbo in *Ninotchka*

   f. June Allyson in *The Opposite Sex*

7. Katharine Hepburn in *The Philadelphia Story*

   g. Greer Garson in *The Law and the Lady*

8. Vivien Leigh in *Waterloo Bridge*

   h. Elizabeth Taylor in *The Girl Who Had Everything*

9. Norma Shearer in *A Free Soul*

   i. Ginger Rogers in *Week-End at the Waldorf*

10. Joan Crawford in *The Last of Mrs. Cheyney*

   j. Cyd Charisse in *Silk Stockings*

122.   Match the performance on the left to its remake on the right.

1. Ginger Rogers in *The Major and the Minor*

2. Maureen O'Hara in *Sentimental Journey*

3. Pat O'Brien in *The Front Page*

4. Alison Skipworth in *Satan Met a Lady*

5. Kay Francis in *One Way Passage*

6. Robert Cummings in *It Started with Eve*

7. Barbara Stanwyck in *The Lady Eve*

8. Carole Lombard in *Nothing Sacred*

9. Bette Davis in *Dark Victory*

10. Betty Grable in *Coney Island*

a. Sydney Greenstreet in *The Maltese Falcon*

b. Jerry Lewis in *Living It Up*

c. Sandra Dee in *I'd Rather Be Rich*

d. Susan Hayward in *Stolen Hours*

e. Merle Oberon in *'Til We Meet Again*

f. Betty Grable in *Wabash Avenue*

g. Jerry Lewis in *You're Never Too Young*

h. Lauren Bacall in *The Gift of Love*

i. Rosalind Russell in *His Girl Friday*

j. Mitzi Gaynor in *The Birds and the Bees*

123.   Match the film to the actress who starred in a remake of that film in the year listed by her name. Some of the remakes kept the original title and some did not.

1. *The Broadway Melody* (1929)

2. *Of Human Bondage* (1934)

3. *Red Dust* (1932)

4. *Libeled Lady* (1936)

5. *A Bill of Divorcement* (1932)

6. *The Maltese Falcon* (1931)

7. *Seventh Heaven* (1927)

8. *20,000 Years in Sing Sing* (1933)

9. *Madame X* (1929)

10. *An American Tragedy* (1931)

a. Ann Sheridan (1940)

b. Simone Simon (1937)

c. Shelley Winters (1951)

d. Ann Sothern (1940)

e. Esther Williams (1946)

f. Eleanor Parker (1946)

g. Bette Davis (1936)

h. Gladys George (1937)

i. Joan Blondell (1940)

j. Maureen O'Hara (1940)

124.   Each actor on the left made a well-known film in the year listed by his name. Match each actor to the one on the right who played the same role in a remake of that film (made in the year listed by his name). How about naming the films too?

1. Charles Laughton (1934)

2. Fredric March (1937)

3. Leslie Howard (1938)

4. Robert Donat (1939)

5. Cary Grant (1940)

6. Melvyn Douglas (1939)

7. Clark Gable (1932)

8. Clark Gable (1935)

9. James Stewart (1940)

10. Wallace Beery (1931)

a. James Mason (1954)

b. Peter O'Toole (1969)

c. Fred Astaire (1957)

d. John Gielgud (1957)

e. Clark Gable (1953)

f. Marlon Brando (1962)

g. Bing Crosby (1956)

h. Rex Harrison (1964)

i. Van Johnson (1949)

j. Jon Voight (1979)

125. Match the Oscar-winning performance on the left to the actor who played the same role in a later film (not necessarily a remake).

1. Charles Coburn in *The More the Merrier*	**a.** Bing Crosby
2. Walter Brennan in *The Westerner*	**b.** Jack Lemmon
3. Thomas Mitchell in *Stagecoach*	**c.** Cesar Romero
4. Warner Baxter in *In Old Arizona*	**d.** William Powell
5. James Stewart in *The Philadelphia Story*	**e.** Cary Grant
6. George Arliss in *Disraeli*	**f.** Robert Shaw
7. Lionel Barrymore in *A Free Soul*	**g.** Alec Guinness
8. Charles Laughton in *The Private Life of Henry VIII*	**h.** Paul Newman
9. Clark Gable in *It Happened One Night*	**i.** Spencer Tracy
10. Fredric March in *Dr. Jekyll and Mr. Hyde*	**j.** Frank Sinatra

126. Match the popular film vehicle to the actor who starred in a 1920s silent version.

1. *The Great Gatsby*	**a.** Rudolph Valentino
2. *Beau Geste*	**b.** Warner Baxter
3. *The Ten Commandments*	**c.** Lewis Stone
4. *Dr. Jekyll and Mr. Hyde*	**d.** Douglas Fairbanks
5. *The Prisoner of Zenda*	**e.** Ronald Colman
6. *The Merry Widow*	**f.** Lon Chaney
7. *Blood and Sand*	**g.** John Barrymore
8. *The Mark of Zorro*	**h.** H. B. Warner
9. *The Hunchback of Notre Dame*	**i.** John Gilbert
10. *The King of Kings*	**j.** Richard Dix

127. Match the comedy to the performer who starred in its musical (or semi-musical) remake. Can you name the remake as well?

1. *Ah, Wilderness!*	**a.** Debbie Reynolds
2. *Ball of Fire*	**b.** Gordon MacRae
3. *It Happened One Night*	**c.** Danny Kaye
4. *Bachelor Mother*	**d.** Dorothy Lamour
5. *Tom, Dick and Harry*	**e.** Deanna Durbin
6. *Midnight*	**f.** Mickey Rooney
7. *Too Many Husbands*	**g.** Betty Grable
8. *The Good Fairy*	**h.** Nelson Eddy
9. *Brother Rat*	**i.** June Allyson
10. *The Guardsman*	**j.** Jane Powell

128. Films are often remade with the same title. Match each title on the left to the years in which two films with that title were released.

1. *My Man Godfrey*	**a.** 1942/1983
2. *Imitation of Life*	**b.** 1935/1954
3. *Magnificent Obsession*	**c.** 1931/1960
4. *To Be or Not to Be*	**d.** 1930/1938
5. *Cimarron*	**e.** 1942/1955
6. *Stagecoach*	**f.** 1936/1957
7. *My Sister Eileen*	**g.** 1932/1957
8. *Holiday*	**h.** 1934/1959
9. *Lost Horizon*	**i.** 1937/1973
10. *A Farewell to Arms*	**j.** 1939/1966

129. Match the film to the description of an earlier, unrelated film with the exact same title.

1. *Carrie* (1976)
2. *No Way Out* (1987)
3. *The Accused* (1988)
4. *The Turning Point* (1977)
5. *Some Like It Hot* (1959)
6. *The Farmer's Daughter* (1947)
7. *The Fugitive* (1993)
8. *Monkey Business* (1952)
9. *A Night to Remember* (1958)
10. *The Sundowners* (1960)

a. 1939 Bob Hope comedy
b. 1949 Loretta Young drama
c. 1950 Robert Preston western
d. 1952 Laurence Olivier drama
e. 1931 Marx Brothers comedy
f. 1950 Richard Widmark drama
g. 1941 Loretta Young comedy
h. 1940 Martha Raye comedy
i. 1952 William Holden drama
j. 1947 Henry Fonda drama

130. Match the actor to the role he played in at least two films.

1. Walter Pidgeon
2. Spencer Tracy
3. Lew Ayres
4. Lewis Stone
5. Mickey Rooney
6. Henry Fonda
7. William Holden
8. William Powell
9. Robert Walker
10. Gordon MacRae

a. James Hardy
b. Bill Seacroft
c. Nick Charles
d. Stanley Banks
e. Marion Hargrove
f. Clem Miniver
g. Frank James
h. Whitey Marsh
i. William Sherman
j. James Kildare

131.   It is rare for a director to remake one of his own hits. Match each filmmaker to the two versions of the same story that he directed.

1. Alfred Hitchcock	**a.** *The Man Who Knew Too Much* (1934 and 1956)
2. Leo McCarey	**b.** *The Strawberry Blonde* (1941); *One Sunday Afternoon* (1948)
3. Frank Capra	**c.** *Destry Rides Again* (1939); *Destry* (1954)
4. William Wyler	**d.** *Midnight* (1939); *Masquerade in Mexico* (1945)
5. Raoul Walsh	**e.** *Lady for a Day* (1933); *Pocketful of Miracles* (1961)
6. Mitchell Leisen	**f.** *The Barretts of Wimpole Street* (1934 and 1957)
7. Howard Hawks	**g.** *Love Affair* (1939); *An Affair to Remember* (1957)
8. Sidney Franklin	**h.** *Ball of Fire* (1941); *A Song Is Born* (1948)
9. George Marshall	**i.** *The Ten Commandments* (1923 and 1956)
10. Cecil B. DeMille	**j.** *These Three* (1936); *The Children's Hour* (1961)

Twelve

I Am a Camera

132. Match the director to one of the jobs he had before he sat in the director's chair.

1. Robert Wise	**a.** Producer of *High Noon*
2. Joseph L. Mankiewicz	**b.** Cast member of *City for Conquest*
3. Elia Kazan	**c.** Co-writer of *Cobra Woman*
4. David Lean	**d.** Costume designer of *The Thief of Bagdad* (1924)
5. Stanley Kramer	**e.** Producer of *The Philadelphia Story*
6. Richard Brooks	**f.** Cast member of *The Best Years of Our Lives*
7. Sam Peckinpah	**g.** Film editor of *Pygmalion*
8. Blake Edwards	**h.** Co-writer of *Jezebel*
9. Mitchell Leisen	**i.** Film editor of *Citizen Kane*
10. John Huston	**j.** Cast member of *Invasion of the Body Snatchers* (1956)

133.   Match the film and one of its directors to the man who co-
    directed it. Some of these pairs worked as teams and some came
    about when one man finished a film started by another.

1. *Singin' in the Rain* –Gene Kelly

2. *Mister Roberts* –Mervyn LeRoy

3. *The Red Shoes* –Emeric Pressburger

4. *In Which We Serve* –David Lean

5. *The Pajama Game* –Stanley Donen

6. *The Court Jester* –Melvin Frank

7. *Come and Get It* –William Wyler

8. *Pygmalion* –Leslie Howard

9. *West Side Story* –Robert Wise

10. *The Adventures of Robin Hood* –
    William Keighley

a. Noël Coward

b. Howard Hawks

c. John Ford

d. Anthony Asquith

e. Stanley Donen

f. Michael Curtiz

g. Jerome Robbins

h. George Abbott

i. Michael Powell

j. Norman Panama

134.   Match the very famous film to the not very famous man who
    directed it.

1. *Sweet Smell of Success*

2. *Gilda*

3. *To Kill a Mockingbird*

4. *This Gun for Hire*

5. *Top Hat*

6. *Pride and Prejudice*

7. *Marty*

8. *For Whom the Bell Tolls*

9. *Now, Voyager*

10. *Pillow Talk*

a. Robert Z. Leonard

b. Frank Tuttle

c. Michael Gordon

d. Sam Wood

e. Alexander Mackendrick

f. Delbert Mann

g. Robert Mulligan

h. Irving Rapper

i. Mark Sandrich

j. Charles Vidor

135.   Match the horror or sci-fi classic to the man who directed it.

1. *I Walked With a Zombie*   **a.** Roman Polanski
2. *Invasion of the Body Snatchers*   **b.** Mark Robson
   (1956)
3. *The Day the Earth Stood Still*   **c.** Andre de Toth
4. *Bride of Frankenstein*   **d.** Tod Browning
5. *Repulsion*   **e.** Robert Wise
6. *House of Wax*   **f.** Don Siegel
7. *Seconds*   **g.** James Whale
8. *Dr. Jekyll and Mr. Hyde* (1932)   **h.** John Frankenheimer
9. *Dracula* (1931)   **i.** Jacques Tourneur
10. *Isle of the Dead*   **j.** Rouben Mamoulian

136.   Match the director to the star he directed in at least four films.

1. Billy Wilder   **a.** Barbara Stanwyck
2. Michael Curtiz   **b.** Miriam Hopkins
3. Cecil B. DeMille   **c.** James Stewart
4. Busby Berkeley   **d.** William Holden
5. Joseph L. Mankiewicz   **e.** Jeanette MacDonald
6. Fritz Lang   **f.** Judy Garland
7. Alfred Hitchcock   **g.** Doris Day
8. Frank Capra   **h.** Rex Harrison
9. William Wyler   **i.** Joan Bennett
10. Ernst Lubitsch   **j.** Gary Cooper

137.   George Cukor hated being called "a woman's director." So let's avoid Kate, Garbo and *The Women* for the moment. Match the actor to the Cukor film in which he appeared.

1. Anthony Quinn	**a.** *Gaslight*
2. Spencer Tracy	**b.** *Susan and God*
3. Ray Milland	**c.** *Holiday*
4. Fredric March	**d.** *Heller in Pink Tights*
5. Melvyn Douglas	**e.** *A Woman's Face*
6. Joseph Cotten	**f.** *Little Women*
7. Stewart Granger	**g.** *A Bill of Divorcement*
8. John Barrymore	**h.** *A Life of Her Own*
9. Lew Ayres	**i.** *Bhowani Junction*
10. Paul Lukas	**j.** *The Actress*

138.   Of course, you can't ignore Great Kate for very long. Match the director to the Katharine Hepburn film he directed.

1. John Ford	**a.** *Suddenly, Last Summer*
2. Gregory La Cava	**b.** *State of the Union*
3. Frank Capra	**c.** *The Sea of Grass*
4. Vincente Minnelli	**d.** *Mary of Scotland*
5. David Lean	**e.** *Woman of the Year*
6. Elia Kazan	**f.** *Bringing Up Baby*
7. Joseph L. Mankiewicz	**g.** *Undercurrent*
8. Howard Hawks	**h.** *Pat and Mike*
9. George Cukor	**i.** *Summertime*
10. George Stevens	**j.** *Stage Door*

139. Match the director to the Gary Cooper film he directed.

1. William A. Wellman	a. *High Noon*
2. Howard Hawks	b. *The Fountainhead*
3. Cecil B. DeMille	c. *They Came to Cordura*
4. Ernst Lubitsch	d. *Friendly Persuasion*
5. Sam Wood	e. *Sergeant York*
6. King Vidor	f. *The Pride of the Yankees*
7. Fred Zinnemann	g. *Beau Geste*
8. William Wyler	h. *The Story of Dr. Wassell*
9. Robert Rossen	i. *Design for Living*
10. Anthony Mann	j. *Man of the West*

140. Match the director to the Marilyn Monroe film he directed.

1. Henry Hathaway	a. *River of No Return*
2. Howard Hawks	b. *Let's Make Love*
3. Joseph L. Mankiewicz	c. *Bus Stop*
4. George Cukor	d. *The Seven Year Itch*
5. Billy Wilder	e. *Monkey Business*
6. Otto Preminger	f. *How to Marry a Millionaire*
7. Fritz Lang	g. *The Asphalt Jungle*
8. Joshua Logan	h. *All About Eve*
9. Jean Negulesco	i. *Clash by Night*
10. John Huston	j. *Niagara*

141.   Match the director to the John Wayne film he directed.

1. John Ford   a. *Sands of Iwo Jima*

2. Howard Hawks   b. *True Grit*

3. John Wayne   c. *Flying Leathernecks*

4. Allan Dwan   d. *The Barbarian and the Geisha*

5. Dick Powell   e. *In Harm's Way*

6. Henry Hathaway   f. *Rio Grande*

7. John Huston   g. *Rio Bravo*

8. William A. Wellman   h. *The Conqueror*

9. Nicholas Ray   i. *The Alamo*

10. Otto Preminger   j. *The High and the Mighty*

Thirteen

I Saw What You Did

142. Match the occupational Rosalind Russell situation to the film in which it appears.

1. She is a judge.	**a.** *She Wouldn't Say Yes*
2. She is an advertising executive.	**b.** *His Girl Friday*
3. She is a literary agent.	**c.** *Design for Scandal*
4. She is a psychiatrist.	**d.** *A Woman of Distinction*
5. She is a reporter.	**e.** *Take a Letter, Darling*
6. She is an aviatrix.	**f.** *Picnic*
7. She is an actress.	**g.** *Flight for Freedom*
8. She is a schoolteacher.	**h.** *This Thing Called Love*
9. She is a college dean.	**i.** *What a Woman*
10. She is an insurance executive.	**j.** *The Velvet Touch*

143.   Match the light comic Cary Grant situation to the film in which it appears.

1. He is engaged to Julia, but ends up with her sister Linda.

   a. *The Bishop's Wife*

2. He must pretend to be Joseph the gardener.

   b. *Arsenic and Old Lace*

3. He announces that he just went gay all of a sudden.

   c. *Holiday*

4. His unearthly powers cause a bottle of sherry to be bottomless.

   d. *The Awful Truth*

5. His soon-to-be ex-wife embarrasses him by pretending to be his floozie sister Lola.

   e. *His Girl Friday*

6. He has been working for *Spy Magazine* ever since his divorce.

   f. *The Talk of the Town*

7. He gets some of his relatives admitted to Happy Dale.

   g. *My Favorite Wife*

8. He tries to come up with an ad slogan for a ham product.

   h. *The Philadelphia Story*

9. He describes his rival Bruce as looking like Ralph Bellamy (Bellamy plays Bruce).

   i. *Bringing Up Baby*

10. He is alarmed to learn that his wife was recently known as Eve to a hunk she called Adam.

   j. *Mr. Blandings Builds His Dream House*

144.   Match the murderous Bette Davis situation to the film in which it appears.

1. She tries to kill her husband and/ or herself in a car crash, but they both survive.

    a. *Dangerous*

2. She causes a large cement urn to fall and crush her cousin and a doctor.

    b. *The Letter*

3. She kills her cleaning woman with a hammer.

    c. *In This Our Life*

4. She kills a child in a hit-and-run accident.

    d. *The Little Foxes*

5. She shoots her lover six times on the front steps.

    e. *Hush ... Hush, Sweet Charlotte*

6. She kills her twin.

    f. *Deception*

7. She kills a great composer (her former lover).

    g. *Beyond the Forest*

8. She causes her husband's death by refusing to bring him his medication.

    h. *What Ever Happened to Baby Jane?*

9. She uses a rifle to kill a man during a hunting trip.

    i. *All This, and Heaven Too*

10. She is imprisoned for complicity in a woman's murder, but is released for lack of evidence.

    j. *Dead Ringer*

145.   Match the outlandish Jack Lemmon situation to the film in which it appears.

1. He goes to jail for the murder of his alter ego (Lord X).

   a. *The Odd Couple*

2. He causes a laundry disaster that buries him in suds.

   b. *The Apartment*

3. He chases (and ultimately rescues) an old woman in a speeding wheelchair.

   c. *The Great Race*

4. He drains spaghetti with a tennis racket.

   d. *Mister Roberts*

5. He confesses to his fiancé that he's not a natural blonde.

   e. *Irma La Douce*

6. He falls head first into a giant cake during a pie fight.

   f. *Bell, Book and Candle*

7. He and his ex-wife try to out-mambo each other at a nightclub.

   g. *Some Like It Hot*

8. His initials are F.U.

   h. *Under the Yum Yum Tree*

9. He is the bongo drum player at the Zodiac Club.

   i. *The Notorious Landlady*

10. He is the lecherous landlord of Centaur Apartments.

   j. *Phffft*

146.   Match the unsavory Barbara Stanwyck situation to the film in which it appears.

1. She walks out on her family and winds up in third-rate vaudeville.

    a. *Double Indemnity*

2. She assumes the identity of a woman killed in a train wreck.

    b. *Baby Face*

3. She throws a pair of scissors into a woman's face.

    c. *California*

4. She tries to prevent her husband from leaving a burning house.

    d. *No Man of Her Own*

5. She and an insurance salesman carry out the murder of her husband.

    e. *All I Desire*

6. She encourages a man to kill her husband, who is unconscious at the foot of a long staircase.

    f. *Remember the Night*

7. She is literally thrown out of town by a group of upstanding women.

    g. *The Violent Men*

8. She steals an expensive bracelet from a jewelry store and is promptly arrested.

    h. *Clash by Night*

9. She sleeps her way to the top of the Gotham Trust Company.

    i. *The Furies*

10. She marries a gentle fisherman but has an affair with his volatile best friend.

    j. *The Strange Love of Martha Ivers*

147.   Match the surprisingly dark James Stewart situation to the film in which it appears.

1. He contemplates suicide on a bridge during a snowstorm.

    a. *Vertigo*

2. He is a doctor wanted by the police for the mercy killing of his wife.

    b. *Bend of the River*

3. He is a bounty hunter passing himself off as a sheriff.

    c. *Rear Window*

4. He has scars on his neck from the time vigilantes tried to hang him.

    d. *It's a Wonderful Life*

5. He kills his brother for the murder of their father.

    e. *The Man from Laramie*

6. He is lassoed and dragged through a campfire.

    f. *The Naked Spur*

7. He loses a leg because of a hunting accident.

    g. *The Far Country*

8. He falls from a window moments after the police save him from a killer.

    h. *The Greatest Show on Earth*

9. He refuses the people of Dawson when they need him to be their marshal.

    i. *The Stratton Story*

10. He forces a brunette to become an exact replica of the blonde he loved and lost.

    j. *Winchester '73*

148.   Match the amusing Claudette Colbert situation to the film in which it appears.

1. Her nightclub act is a triumph of personality over musical skills.

    a. *Without Reservations*

2. Despite her royal blood, she takes work as a housemaid.

    b. *The Palm Beach Story*

3. She is a poet who does some amateur sleuthing.

    c. *The Gilded Lily*

4. She is a novelist traveling to Hollywood by train.

    d. *Midnight*

5. She escapes her father by diving off his yacht.

    e. *It Happened One Night*

6. The Wienie King gets her out of debt.

    f. *Tovarich*

7. She purposely eats raw scallions to discourage her husband's amorous advances.

    g. *It's a Wonderful World*

8. She uses paint to write "I'm Through!" on a wall.

    h. *Arise, My Love*

9. She is stranded in Paris with nothing but her evening gown.

    i. *Bluebeard's Eighth Wife*

10. She pretends to be the wife of an imprisoned flyer.

    j. *The Egg and I*

149. Match the intense situation to the film about mental illness in which it appears.

1. A man throws a typewriter at his wife which smashes her hand.

2. A woman sits quietly in a boat as her brother-in-law drowns nearby.

3. A woman fears she has inherited her father's insanity and opts for celibacy.

4. A woman wanders the streets of L.A. asking strangers for David.

5. A man cannot bear to see rows of lines on white backgrounds.

6. A woman recalls a childhood incident in which she was forced to kiss her dead grandmother goodbye.

7. A woman recalls a childhood incident in which she wished her father would die and he did.

8. A woman tries to secure an unnecessary lobotomy for her niece.

9. A brilliant doctor poisons his troubled daughter and then shoots himself.

10. A young man has a public breakdown due to pressure from his impossible-to-please father.

a. *Possessed* (1947)

b. *A Bill of Divorcement*

c. *Kings Row*

d. *Autumn Leaves*

e. *The Snake Pit*

f. *Leave Her to Heaven*

g. *Suddenly, Last Summer*

h. *Spellbound*

i. *Fear Strikes Out*

j. *The Three Faces of Eve*

150.   Smoking may be increasingly prohibited in American life, but can you imagine the movies without cigarettes? Match the cigarette-related event to the movie in which it appears.

1. A woman's cigarette is put out in a jar of cold cream.

2. A woman's cigarette is put out in the yolk of a fried egg.

3. A woman's cigarette is put out in a nun's hand.

4. A widow smokes from under her mourning veil.

5. A lounge singer stains her piano by placing lit cigarettes on top of it whenever she plays.

6. A woman's cigarette (in a very long holder) sets another woman's hat on fire.

7. A man lights two cigarettes in his mouth (one is for Charlotte Vale).

8. A man's cigarette is put out in a raw oyster.

9. A man uses his lit cigarette to pop a child's balloon at an amusement park.

10. A man lights his lover's cigarette by pressing the lit one in his mouth against the unlit one in hers.

a. *Now, Voyager*

b. *Strangers on a Train*

c. *Fanny* (1961)

d. *Love Is a Many-Splendored Thing*

e. *Suddenly, Last Summer*

f. *Rebecca*

g. *Road House*

h. *Breakfast at Tiffany's*

i. *To Catch a Thief*

j. *Stage Fright*

151.   Match the imaginative lipstick-related event to the film in which it appears.

1. A woman writes "No Sale" in lipstick on a mirror.

   a. *Destry Rides Again*

2. A woman uses lipstick to write her initials (C.P.) on a man's chest.

   b. *Saboteur*

3. A woman uses lipstick to put a mustache on a movie mogul's plaque.

   c. *The Hustler*

4. A woman throws an S.O.S. note written in lipstick out a skyscraper window.

   d. *On Her Majesty's Secret Service*

5. A woman uses lipstick to write a message on the nightgown she is wearing and then throws herself out a window.

   e. *Butterfield 8*

6. A woman uses lipstick to write her suicide note on a bathroom mirror: "Perverted Twisted Crippled."

   f. *The Bad and the Beautiful*

7. A woman wipes off her lipstick using her bare hand and her feather boa.

   g. *Lifeboat*

8. A lipstick tube rolling on the floor marks the entrance of Cora.

   h. *A Star Is Born* (1954)

9. A man uses lipstick to write the initials E.B. and N.M. (in a heart) on a backstage wall.

   i. *Three on a Match*

10. A woman uses lipstick to write her room number on a man's thigh.

   j. *The Postman Always Rings Twice* (1946)

Fourteen

Author! Author!

152. Match the playwright to the film for which he/she wrote the screenplay.

1. Moss Hart   **a.** *The Best Years of Our Lives*

2. Garson Kanin   **b.** *Gone With the Wind*

3. Robert E. Sherwood   **c.** *It Should Happen to You*

4. Ben Hecht   **d.** *The Manchurian Candidate* (1962)

5. Paddy Chayefsky   **e.** *Dead End*

6. Lillian Hellman   **f.** *A Star Is Born* (1954)

7. Paul Osborn   **g.** *The Goddess*

8. Sidney Howard   **h.** *Splendor in the Grass*

9. William Inge   **i.** *Notorious*

10. George Axelrod   **j.** *East of Eden*

153. Match the film on the left to the play or musical on the right that we see rehearsed and/or performed in the film (in one of them, we see only the curtain call).

1. *Auntie Mame*   **a.** *The Young Sarah*
2. *All About Eve*   **b.** *The Land Around Us*
3. *The Country Girl*   **c.** *Halfway to Heaven*
4. *Stage Door*   **d.** *Othello*
5. *The Barkleys of Broadway*   **e.** *Pretty Lady*
6. *Twentieth Century*   **f.** *Enchanted April*
7. *A Double Life*   **g.** *Midsummer Madness*
8. *Dangerous*   **h.** *But to Die*
9. *Sudden Fear*   **i.** *Aged in Wood*
10. *42nd Street*   **j.** *The Heart of Kentucky*

154. Match the writer to the film for which he/she wrote or co-wrote the screenplay.

1. Aldous Huxley   **a.** *Suddenly, Last Summer*
2. Truman Capote   **b.** *Easter Parade*
3. Dorothy Parker   **c.** *Beat the Devil*
4. Sidney Sheldon   **d.** *Moby Dick* (1956)
5. John Steinbeck   **e.** *To Have and Have Not*
6. Gore Vidal   **f.** *Pride and Prejudice* (1940)
7. F. Scott Fitzgerald   **g.** *The Night of the Hunter*
8. William Faulkner   **h.** *A Star Is Born* (1937)
9. James Agee   **i.** *Three Comrades*
10. Ray Bradbury   **j.** *Viva Zapata!*

155.   Match the film on the left to the fictional book on the right that is written by a character in the film.

1. *Theodora Goes Wild*
2. *The Ghost and Mrs. Muir*
3. *Suspicion*
4. *Auntie Mame*
5. *Cluny Brown*
6. *The Bad and the Beautiful*
7. *Arsenic and Old Lace*
8. *Spellbound*
9. *The Seven Year Itch*
10. *Old Acquaintance*

a. *The Nightingale Murder!*
b. *The Sinner*
c. *Of Man and the Unconscious*
d. *Blood and Swash*
e. *Marriage, a Fraud and a Failure*
f. *Labyrinth of the Guilt Complex*
g. *Murder on the Footbridge*
h. *Married in June*
i. *Live! Live! Live!*
j. *A Woman of Taste*

156.   Match the star to his/her autobiography.

1. Gene Tierney
2. Alec Guinness
3. Joan Fontaine
4. Joseph Cotten
5. Katharine Hepburn
6. Dirk Bogarde
7. Bette Davis
8. Mary Astor
9. Lilli Palmer
10. Janet Leigh

a. *Vanity Will Get You Somewhere*
b. *Change Lobsters and Dance*
c. *The Lonely Life*
d. *Blessings in Disguise*
e. *Snakes & Ladders*
f. *There Really Was a Hollywood*
g. *Self-Portrait*
h. *A Life on Film*
i. *No Bed of Roses*
j. *Me*

Fifteen

Man Hunt

Hint: Again, each star has 5 correct answers.

157.   Charlie Chaplin or Buster Keaton?

1. Who directed the 1923 drama *A Woman of Paris?*
2. Who was a Best Actor nominee at the first Academy Awards?
3. Who appeared in *Around the World in Eighty Days?*
4. Who was under contract to MGM?
5. Who appeared as himself in the 1928 Marion Davies comedy *Show People?*
6. Who won a N.Y. Film Critics Award for acting?
7. Whose *Three Ages* was a spoof of *Intolerance?*
8. Who appeared in the all-star picture *The Hollywood Revue of 1929?*
9. Who directed and appeared with Martha Raye in a 1947 film?
10. Who made a cameo appearance in *Sunset Boulevard?*

158.   Humphrey Bogart or Edward G. Robinson?

1. Who won a Best Actor Oscar?
2. Who received a posthumous honorary Oscar?
3. Who starred in *The Return of Dr. X*?
4. Who recreated his 1935 Broadway triumph in a 1936 film?
5. Who starred in two Fritz Lang films?
6. Who starred in a film directed by Orson Welles?
7. Who starred with Barbara Stanwyck in *The Violent Men*?
8. Who starred with June Allyson in *Battle Circus*?
9. Who dies at the end of *Key Largo*?
10. Who appeared in two William Wyler films?

159.   Clark Gable or Spencer Tracy?

1. Who dies at the end of *Test Pilot*?
2. Who marries Claudette Colbert in *Boom Town*?
3. Whose last film was directed by John Huston?
4. Who starred with Garbo in *Susan Lenox (Her Fall and Rise)*?
5. Who teamed with Rosalind Russell in *They Met in Bombay*?
6. Who teamed with Joan Crawford in *Mannequin*?
7. Who was Oscar-nominated for *San Francisco*?
8. Who starred in a western directed by Elia Kazan?
9. Who joined Myrna Loy and William Powell in *Libeled Lady*?
10. Who joined Myrna Loy and William Powell in *Manhattan Melodrama*?

160.   Cary Grant or James Stewart?

1. Who starred in a remake of the silent *Seventh Heaven*?
2. Who made two films with Ginger Rogers?
3. Who marries Katharine Hepburn at the end of *The Philadelphia Story*?
4. Who starred with Joan Crawford in *The Ice Follies of 1939*?
5. Who starred with Deborah Kerr in *Dream Wife*?
6. Who appeared in one of the Jeanette MacDonald/Nelson Eddy operettas?
7. Who played Roger Thornhill in a Hitchcock thriller?
8. Who teamed with Rosalind Russell in *No Time for Comedy*?
9. Who played the male lead in the musical extravaganza *Ziegfeld Girl*?
10. Who played Leopold Dilg in a 1942 Oscar nominee for Best Picture?

161.   Errol Flynn or Tyrone Power?

1. Who played Jake Barnes in *The Sun Also Rises*?
2. Who starred in *Prince of Foxes* and *Son of Fury*?
3. Who starred in *Virginia City* and *San Antonio*?
4. Who fought World War II in *Desperate Journey*?
5. Who fought World War II in *Crash Dive*?
6. Who starred with Maureen O'Hara in *The Black Swan*?
7. Who starred with Maureen O'Hara in *Against All Flags*?
8. Who played Greer Garson's husband in *That Forsyte Woman*?
9. Who starred in Rudyard Kipling's *Kim* with Dean Stockwell?
10. Who was replaced by Yul Brynner when he died during the filming of *Solomon and Sheba*?

162.   Joel McCrea or Randolph Scott?

1. Who starred in a western remake of *High Sierra*?

2. Who appeared in two musicals with Fred Astaire?

3. Who starred with Helen Gahagan in the 1935 camp classic *She*?

4. Who romanced Jean Arthur in *The More the Merrier*?

5. Who starred as *Buffalo Bill*, *The Virginian* and Wyatt Earp in *Wichita*?

6. Who made two films with Marlene Dietrich in 1942?

7. Who starred in Alfred Hitchcock's *Foreign Correspondent*?

8. Who got caught between Irene Dunne and Cary Grant in *My Favorite Wife*?

9. Who starred with Barbara Stanwyck in DeMille's *Union Pacific*?

10. Who played Gil Westrum in *Ride the High Country*?

163.   Fred Astaire or Gene Kelly?

1. Who starred in the modest musical *Living in a Big Way*?

2. Who starred in a musical directed by George Cukor?

3. Who starred in a musical directed by Francis Ford Coppola?

4. Who paired with June Allyson in a 1948 film?

5. Who was the first to star in a Vincente Minnelli musical?

6. Who introduced an Oscar-winning song?

7. Whose first film was directed by Busby Berkeley?

8. Who was in Stanley Donen's first solo directorial effort?

9. Who danced in a Roland Petit ballet with Leslie Caron in a 1955 musical?

10. Who made a cameo in the Marilyn Monroe musical *Let's Make Love*?

164.   Alec Guinness or Laurence Olivier?

1. Who appeared with Irene Dunne in *The Mudlark*?

2. Who had a featured role in *Doctor Zhivago*?

3. Who starred with Simone Signoret in *Term of Trial*?

4. Who teamed with John Mills in *Tunes of Glory*?

5. Who appeared with Bette Davis in *The Scapegoat*?

6. Who played The Mahdi in *Khartoum* with Charlton Heston?

7. Who played the inspector in *Bunny Lake Is Missing*?

8. Who played Sophia Loren's father in *The Fall of the Roman Empire*?

9. Who found Tony Curtis irresistible in the restored version of a 1960 epic?

10. Who appeared with Kirk Douglas and Burt Lancaster in *The Devil's Disciple*?

165.   Kirk Douglas or Burt Lancaster?

1. Who starred in a 1951 Billy Wilder drama with Jan Sterling?

2. Who made films with Tony Curtis in 1956 and 1957?

3. Who played the villain in *Seven Days in May*?

4. Whose first film starred Barbara Stanwyck?

5. Who appeared with Rosalind Russell in *Mourning Becomes Electra*?

6. Who starred in three Vincente Minnelli films?

7. Who won a Best Actor Oscar?

8. Who starred with Audrey Hepburn in a 1960 western?

9. Who starred with Gary Cooper in the 1954 western *Vera Cruz*?

10. Who played Doc Holliday in *Gunfight at the O.K. Corral*?

166.   Marlon Brando or Montgomery Clift?

1. Who starred in a 1954 Vittorio De Sica film?

2. Who starred with Sophia Loren in a film directed by Charlie Chaplin?

3. Who starred in an Alfred Hitchcock film?

4. Who starred in a Howard Hawks western?

5. Who made his screen debut opposite Teresa Wright?

6. Who starred in a comedy with Shirley Jones?

7. Who starred in the 1953 Oscar-winning Best Picture?

8. Who starred in the 1954 Oscar-winning Best Picture?

9. Who appeared in a 1961 film with an original screenplay by Arthur Miller?

10. Who played Christian Diestl in *The Young Lions*?

Sixteen

Let's Dance

167. Match the dancer or dancing team to the musical in which he/she/they performed.

1. The Nicholas Brothers	**a.** *Li'l Abner*
2. Bob Fosse	**b.** *Les Girls*
3. Marge and Gower Champion	**c.** *Hit the Deck* (1955)
4. Vera-Ellen	**d.** *The Pirate*
5. Cyd Charisse	**e.** *April in Paris*
6. Mitzi Gaynor	**f.** *Damn Yankees*
7. Julie Newmar	**g.** *Call Me Madam*
8. Ray Bolger	**h.** *Singin' in the Rain*
9. James Cagney	**i.** *Lovely to Look At*
10. Russ Tamblyn	**j.** *The Seven Little Foys*

168.   Match the remarkable (and sometimes groundbreaking) dance sequence to the musical in which it appears.

1. "From This Moment On"	**a.** *Born to Dance*
2. "Girl Hunt"	**b.** *Ziegfeld Follies*
3. "Swingin' the Jinx Away"	**c.** *Kiss Me Kate*
4. "Frankie and Johnny"	**d.** *Words and Music*
5. "Slaughter on 10th Avenue"	**e.** *Easter Parade*
6. "Limehouse Blues"	**f.** *Royal Wedding*
7. "Let's Say It with Firecrackers"	**g.** *Meet Me in Las Vegas*
8. "You're All the World to Me"	**h.** *The Band Wagon*
9. "The Barn-Raising Dance"	**i.** *Holiday Inn*
10. "Steppin' Out With My Baby"	**j.** *Seven Brides for Seven Brothers*

169.   Match the choreographer to the musical for which he/she created the dances. In some of these instances, the choreographers adapted work they had originated on Broadway.

1. Bob Fosse	**a.** *The Band Wagon*
2. Michael Kidd	**b.** *Brigadoon*
3. Agnes de Mille	**c.** *The Pajama Game*
4. Gene Kelly	**d.** *Top Hat*
5. Roland Petit	**e.** *Gentlemen Prefer Blondes*
6. Jack Cole	**f.** *Easter Parade*
7. Hermes Pan	**g.** *Oliver!*
8. Jerome Robbins	**h.** *Oklahoma!*
9. Onna White	**i.** *The King and I*
10. Robert Alton	**j.** *Hans Christian Andersen*

170.   Match the Fred Astaire dance number to the woman who was his partner. Then name the film.

1. "Heigh Ho, the Gang's All Here"	**a.** Ginger Rogers
2. "Begin the Beguine"	**b.** Lucille Bremer
3. "This Heart of Mine"	**c.** Eleanor Powell
4. "It Only Happens When I Dance with You"	**d.** Leslie Caron
5. "I'm Old-Fashioned"	**e.** Audrey Hepburn
6. "Pick Yourself Up"	**f.** Joan Crawford
7. "Something's Gotta Give"	**g.** Jane Powell
8. "I Left My Hat in Haiti"	**h.** Cyd Charisse
9. "All of You"	**i.** Rita Hayworth
10. "He Loves and She Loves"	**j.** Ann Miller

171.   Match the male performer to the musical number in which he danced (or at least moved well) with Gene Kelly. Then name the film.

1. Frank Sinatra	**a.** "I Begged Her"
2. Van Johnson	**b.** "Make Way for Tomorrow"
3. Phil Silvers	**c.** "The Worry Song"
4. Donald O'Connor	**d.** "The Babbitt and the Bromide"
5. Dan Dailey	**e.** "Moses Supposes"
6. Georges Guetary	**f.** "The Alter Ego Dance"
7. Fred Kelly (his brother)	**g.** "March, March"
8. Fred Astaire	**h.** "'S Wonderful"
9. Jerry the Mouse	**i.** "I'll Go Home with Bonnie Jean"
10. Gene Kelly	**j.** "I Love to Go Swimmin' with Women"

Seventeen
Oh, Men! Oh, Women!

172. Match the actress to the film in which she appeared with either Fredric March or William Powell.

1. Esther Williams	a. *Dr. Jekyll and Mr. Hyde* with Fredric March
2. Joan Bennett	b. *Fashions of 1934* with William Powell
3. Jean Harlow	c. *The Affairs of Cellini* with Fredric March
4. Ann Blyth	d. *The Heavenly Body* with William Powell
5. Fay Wray	e. *Trade Winds* with Fredric March
6. Bette Davis	f. *The Hoodlum Saint* with William Powell
7. Hedy Lamarr	g. *Smilin' Through* with Fredric March
8. Norma Shearer	h. *Reckless* with William Powell
9. Miriam Hopkins	i. *The Dark Angel* with Fredric March
10. Merle Oberon	j. *Mr. Peabody and the Mermaid* with William Powell

173.   Match the actor to the film in which he appeared with either Susan Hayward or Gene Tierney.

1. Clark Gable	a. *Ada* with Susan Hayward
2. Henry Fonda	b. *Plymouth Adventure* with Gene Tierney
3. Tyrone Power	c. *White Witch Doctor* with Susan Hayward
4. Spencer Tracy	d. *The Left Hand of God* with Gene Tierney
5. Gary Cooper	e. *Untamed* with Susan Hayward
6. Dean Martin	f. *Never Let Me Go* with Gene Tierney
7. Humphrey Bogart	g. *The President's Lady* with Susan Hayward
8. Robert Mitchum	h. *Rings on Her Fingers* with Gene Tierney
9. Dana Andrews	i. *Garden of Evil* with Susan Hayward
10. Charlton Heston	j. *The Iron Curtain* with Gene Tierney

174.   Match the actress to the film in which she appeared with either Fred MacMurray or Ray Milland.

1. Jean Arthur	a. *The Lady Is Willing* with Fred MacMurray
2. Claudette Colbert	b. *Kitty* with Ray Milland
3. Barbara Stanwyck	c. *Above Suspicion* with Fred MacMurray
4. Loretta Young	d. *Copper Canyon* with Ray Milland
5. Marlene Dietrich	e. *There's Always Tomorrow* with Fred MacMurray
6. Carole Lombard	f. *Easy Living* with Ray Milland
7. Irene Dunne	g. *Hands Across the Table* with Fred MacMurray
8. Hedy Lamarr	h. *The Doctor Takes a Wife* with Ray Milland
9. Paulette Goddard	i. *Never a Dull Moment* with Fred MacMurray
10. Joan Crawford	j. *Skylark* with Ray Milland

175. Match the actor to the film in which he appeared with either Lauren Bacall or Rita Hayworth.

1. Richard Widmark

2. William Powell

3. Glenn Ford

4. Gary Cooper

5. Burt Lancaster

6. Victor Mature

7. Fred MacMurray

8. Stewart Granger

9. Robert Mitchum

10. John Wayne

a. *How to Marry a Millionaire* with Lauren Bacall

b. *My Gal Sal* with Rita Hayworth

c. *Blood Alley* with Lauren Bacall

d. *Salome* with Rita Hayworth

e. *Woman's World* with Lauren Bacall

f. *The Loves of Carmen* with Rita Hayworth

g. *The Cobweb* with Lauren Bacall

h. *Fire Down Below* with Rita Hayworth

i. *Bright Leaf* with Lauren Bacall

j. *Separate Tables* with Rita Hayworth

176. Match the actress to the film in which she appeared with either Alan Ladd or Robert Mitchum.

1. Dorothy Lamour

2. Linda Darnell

3. Janet Leigh

4. Geraldine Fitzgerald

5. Loretta Young

6. Shelley Winters

7. Gail Russell

8. Eleanor Parker

9. Virginia Mayo

10. Olivia de Havilland

a. *Salty O'Rourke* with Alan Ladd

b. *Home from the Hill* with Robert Mitchum

c. *China* with Alan Ladd

d. *Second Chance* with Robert Mitchum

e. *Wild Harvest* with Alan Ladd

f. *Not As a Stranger* with Robert Mitchum

g. *O. S. S.* with Alan Ladd

h. *The Night of the Hunter* with Robert Mitchum

i. *The Iron Mistress* with Alan Ladd

j. *Holiday Affair* with Robert Mitchum

177.   Match the actor to the film in which he appeared with either Jennifer Jones or Deborah Kerr.

1. John Garfield

2. Gary Cooper

3. Charles Boyer

4. David Niven

5. Spencer Tracy

6. Montgomery Clift

7. William Eythe

8. Yul Brynner

9. Louis Jourdan

10. Clark Gable

a. *Madame Bovary* with Jennifer Jones

b. *Edward, My Son* with Deborah Kerr

c. *We Were Strangers* with Jennifer Jones

d. *The Hucksters* with Deborah Kerr

e. *Indiscretion of an American Wife* with Jennifer Jones

f. *The Naked Edge* with Deborah Kerr

g. *Cluny Brown* with Jennifer Jones

h. *The Journey* with Deborah Kerr

i. *The Song of Bernadette* with Jennifer Jones

j. *Bonjour Tristesse* with Deborah Kerr

Eighteen
The Professionals

178. Have you been paying attention to the opening credits? Match the film industry employee to his/her skill.

1. Sydney Guilaroff	**a.** producing
2. Natalie Kalmus	**b.** screenwriting
3. Margaret Booth	**c.** cinematography
4. Harry Stradling	**d.** art direction
5. Dorothy Jeakins	**e.** film editing
6. Douglas Shearer	**f.** costume design
7. Franz Waxman	**g.** composing scores
8. Dalton Trumbo	**h.** Technicolor color direction
9. Pandro S. Berman	**i.** hair styling
10. Cedric Gibbons	**j.** sound recording

179.   The year 1939 is usually regarded as Hollywood's peak. Let us give some of the credit where credit is due...in the credits. Match the '39 classic to its corresponding credit.

1. *The Women*
2. *Gunga Din*
3. *Ninotchka*
4. *Of Mice and Men*
5. *Destry Rides Again*
6. *Wuthering Heights*
7. *The Wizard of Oz*
8. *Only Angels Have Wings*
9. *Stagecoach*
10. *Gone With the Wind*

a. Produced by Mervyn LeRoy
b. Co-written by Billy Wilder
c. Lyrics by Frank Loesser
d. Directed by George Stevens
e. Produced by Samuel Goldwyn
f. Featuring Rita Hayworth
g. Featuring Paulette Goddard
h. Screenplay by Dudley Nichols
i. Directed by Lewis Milestone
j. Photographed by Ernest Haller

180.   Match the acclaimed film to its great cinematographer.

1. *Citizen Kane*
2. *Touch of Evil*
3. *Vertigo*
4. *Queen Christina*
5. *Casablanca*
6. *The Magnificent Ambersons*
7. *From Here to Eternity*
8. *The Searchers*
9. *The African Queen*
10. *Hud*

a. Stanley Cortez
b. James Wong Howe
c. Russell Metty
d. Burnett Guffey
e. Gregg Toland
f. William Daniels
g. Jack Cardiff
h. Arthur Edeson
i. Robert Burks
j. Winton C. Hoch

181. Here's one for those of you who get excited by a "Gowns by..." credit. Match the memorably costumed film to its celebrated designer.

1. *Gone With the Wind*	**a**. Adrian
2. *The Wizard of Oz*	**b**. Helen Rose
3. *Gigi*	**c**. Irene Sharaff
4. *Gilda*	**d**. Orry-Kelly
5. *The Scarlet Empress*	**e**. Travilla
6. *A Place in the Sun*	**f**. Jean Louis
7. *The Bad and the Beautiful*	**g**. Walter Plunkett
8. *The King and I*	**h**. Travis Banton
9. *Auntie Mame*	**i**. Edith Head
10. *Gentlemen Prefer Blondes*	**j**. Cecil Beaton

182. Match the composer to the film for which he wrote the score.

1. Leonard Bernstein	**a**. *The Heiress*
2. Max Steiner	**b**. *The High and the Mighty*
3. Aaron Copland	**c**. *Anatomy of a Murder*
4. David Raksin	**d**. *Laura*
5. Erich Wolfgang Korngold	**e**. *Citizen Kane*
6. Bernard Herrmann	**f**. *On the Waterfront*
7. Dimitri Tiomkin	**g**. *Kings Row*
8. Ernest Gold	**h**. *Spellbound*
9. Duke Ellington	**i**. *Now, Voyager*
10. Miklos Rozsa	**j**. *Exodus*

Nineteen
Change of Habit

183. Match the musical performer to the film in which he/she played a dramatic role.

1. Judy Garland   **a.** *Christmas Holiday*
2. Esther Williams   **b.** *Little Boy Lost*
3. Debbie Reynolds   **c.** *A Child Is Waiting*
4. Dick Powell   **d.** *Cornered*
5. Bing Crosby   **e.** *I Wake Up Screaming*
6. Betty Grable   **f.** *The Catered Affair*
7. Gene Kelly   **g.** *The Young Lions*
8. Doris Day   **h.** *Storm Warning*
9. Dean Martin   **i.** *Twilight for the Gods*
10. Cyd Charisse   **j.** *The Unguarded Moment*

184.   Match the usually nonmusical performer to the musical in which he/she sang and/or danced (sometimes rather well and sometimes blessedly briefly).

1. Claudette Colbert	**a.** *The Harvey Girls*
2. Louis Calhern	**b.** *Broadway Melody of 1936*
3. Arlene Dahl	**c.** *The Smiling Lieutenant*
4. Walter Huston	**d.** *Silk Stockings*
5. Paulette Goddard	**e.** *Call Me Madam*
6. Robert Taylor	**f.** *Second Chorus*
7. Marjorie Main	**g.** *Annie Get Your Gun*
8. George Sanders	**h.** *Les Girls*
9. Kay Kendall	**i.** *Yankee Doodle Dandy*
10. Peter Lorre	**j.** *Three Little Words*

185.   Match the silent star to the talking picture in which he/she played a supporting role.

1. Lillian Gish	**a.** *In the Good Old Summertime*
2. Richard Barthelmess	**b.** *The Unforgiven*
3. Dolores Costello	**c.** *Since You Went Away*
4. Buster Keaton	**d.** *Only Angels Have Wings*
5. Alla Nazimova	**e.** *The Searchers*
6. Conrad Nagel	**f.** *Sabrina* (1954)
7. Jackie Coogan	**g.** *The Magnificent Ambersons*
8. Ramon Novarro	**h.** *Heller in Pink Tights*
9. Antonio Moreno	**i.** *The Joker Is Wild*
10. Francis X. Bushman	**j.** *All That Heaven Allows*

186. Match the television star to the film in which he/she appeared before fame hit on the small screen.

1. Ted Knight
2. Carroll O'Connor
3. Cloris Leachman

4. June Lockhart
5. George Reeves
6. Robert Blake
7. Jack Klugman
8. Jack Webb
9. Fred Gwynne
10. Raymond Burr

a. *Cleopatra* (1963)
b. *On the Waterfront*
c. *The Treasure of the Sierra Madre*
d. *Psycho*
e. *12 Angry Men*
f. *Meet Me in St. Louis*
g. *A Place in the Sun*
h. *Gone With the Wind*
i. *Kiss Me Deadly*
j. *Sunset Boulevard*

187. Match the Hollywood performer to the European film in which he/she appeared.

1. Burt Lancaster
2. Jean Seberg
3. Farley Granger
4. George Sanders
5. Lex Barker
6. Steve Cochran
7. Jack Palance
8. Mel Ferrer
9. Richard Basehart
10. Louise Brooks

a. *La Strada*
b. *Il Grido*
c. *Elena et les Hommes*
d. *Breathless*
e. *Contempt*
f. *Viaggio in Italia*
g. *Diary of a Lost Girl*
h. *Senso*
i. *The Leopard*
j. *La Dolce Vita*

188. Match the international star to the American film in which he/she appeared.

1. Anna Magnani	a. *Ship of Fools*
2. Max von Sydow	b. *The Train*
3. Simone Signoret	c. *My Geisha*
4. Toshiro Mifune	d. *5 Fingers*
5. Danielle Darrieux	e. *All That Money Can Buy*
6. Cantinflas	f. *Hell in the Pacific*
7. Jeanne Moreau	g. *Hawaii*
8. Yves Montand	h. *Rhapsody*
9. Vittorio Gassman	i. *Pepe*
10. Simone Simon	j. *Wild Is the Wind*

189. Match the film professional (primarily known for something other than writing) to the film for which he/she wrote or contributed to the story and/or screenplay.

1. Frank Capra	a. *Since You Went Away*
2. Rosalind Russell	b. *Thunder Road*
3. Robert Mitchum	c. *The Horse's Mouth*
4. David O. Selznick	d. *Adam's Rib*
5. Burgess Meredith	e. *Monsieur Verdoux*
6. Ruth Gordon	f. *The Unguarded Moment*
7. Alec Guinness	g. *Private Hell 36*
8. Ida Lupino	h. *Take Me Out to the Ball Game*
9. Stanley Donen	i. *Westward the Women*
10. Orson Welles	j. *The Diary of a Chambermaid* (1946)

190.   Match the performer to the film he/she directed.

1. Gower Champion	a. *The Enemy Below*
2. Peter Ustinov	b. *The Gallant Hours*
3. Ida Lupino	c. *The Man on the Eiffel Tower*
4. Gene Kelly	d. *Hello, Dolly!*
5. Burgess Meredith	e. *My Six Loves*
6. Gene Nelson	f. *State Fair* (1962)
7. Robert Montgomery	g. *Billy Budd*
8. Dick Powell	h. *The Buccaneer* (1958)
9. Jose Ferrer	i. *The Hitch-Hiker*
10. Anthony Quinn	j. *Harum Scarum*

191.   Match the director or choreographer to the film in which he appeared in an acting role.

1. Gregory Ratoff	a. *It's Always Fair Weather*
2. Vittorio De Sica	b. *Five Graves to Cairo*
3. John Huston	c. *A Farewell to Arms* (1957)
4. Michael Kidd	d. *Never on Sunday*
5. Preston Sturges	e. *Stalag 17*
6. Jules Dassin	f. *Hold Back the Dawn*
7. Jack Cole	g. *All About Eve*
8. Erich von Stroheim	h. *Paris Holiday*
9. Otto Preminger	i. *The Cardinal*
10. Mitchell Leisen	j. *Designing Woman*

192.   Match the usually nonmusical director to the musical film he directed.

1. Henry King	a. *Swing Time*
2. William Wyler	b. *Gentlemen Prefer Blondes*
3. Fred Zinnemann	c. *Show Boat* (1936)
4. Howard Hawks	d. *Funny Girl*
5. Michael Curtiz	e. *Guys and Dolls*
6. George Stevens	f. *Mary Poppins*
7. Joseph L. Mankiewicz	g. *Carousel*
8. Otto Preminger	h. *White Christmas*
9. James Whale	i. *Oklahoma!*
10. Robert Stevenson	j. *Carmen Jones*

193.   Match the director (most often associated with musicals) to one of the nonmusical films he directed.

1. Vincente Minnelli	a. *The Three Musketeers* (1948)
2. Busby Berkeley	b. *Desk Set*
3. Rouben Mamoulian	c. *The Long, Long Trailer*
4. Roy Del Ruth	d. *The Tender Trap*
5. Stanley Donen	e. *So Proudly We Hail!*
6. Irving Cummings	f. *The Maltese Falcon* (1931)
7. George Sidney	g. *They Made Me a Criminal*
8. Charles Walters	h. *Golden Boy*
9. Mark Sandrich	i. *The Story of Alexander Graham Bell*
10. Walter Lang	j. *Charade*

Twenty

Stardust Memories

194. Match the actor on the left to the movie star he played in a film.

1. Rod Steiger	**a.** Al Jolson
2. James Cagney	**b.** Eddie Cantor
3. Kevin Kline	**c.** Lon Chaney
4. Larry Parks	**d.** George Raft
5. Errol Flynn	**e.** Bela Lugosi
6. Ray Danton	f. W.C. Fields
7. Donald O'Connor	**g.** John Barrymore
8. Keefe Brasselle	**h.** Douglas Fairbanks
9. Martin Landau	**i.** Clark Gable
10. James Brolin	**j.** Buster Keaton

195.   Pick the star's one black-and-white film in each group.

1. Errol Flynn
   a. *Dive Bomber*; **b.** *Adventures of Don Juan*; **c.** *The Sea Hawk*; **d.** *Dodge City*

2. Ingrid Bergman
   a. *Joan of Arc*; **b.** *Saratoga Trunk*; **c.** *Anastasia*; **d.** *Indiscreet*

3. James Stewart
   a. *Winchester '73*; **b.** *Broken Arrow*; **c.** *The Naked Spur*; **d.** *Two Rode Together*

4. Rita Hayworth
   a. *My Gal Sal*; **b.** *Fire Down Below*; **c.** *The Loves of Carmen*; **d.** *Affair in Trinidad*

5. Gary Cooper
   a. *North West Mounted Police*; **b.** *Unconquered*; **c.** *The Adventures of Marco Polo*; **d.** *Friendly Persuasion*

6. Susan Hayward
   a. *The Lusty Men*; **b.** *With a Song in My Heart*; **c.** *Canyon Passage*; **d.** *Soldier of Fortune*

7. John Wayne
   a. *Hondo*; **b.** *The Horse Soldiers*; **c.** *Rio Bravo*; **d.** *Rio Grande*

8. Audrey Hepburn
   a. *Green Mansions*; **b.** *Love in the Afternoon*; **c.** *Charade*; **d.** *The Nun's Story*

9. Nelson Eddy
   a. *Sweethearts*; **b.** *Maytime*; **c.** *Bitter Sweet*; **d.** *The Phantom of the Opera*

10. Deborah Kerr
   a. *The Sundowners*; **b.** *Heaven Knows, Mr. Allison*; **c.** *Separate Tables*; **d.** *The Grass Is Greener*

196.   Pick the star's one color film in each group.

1. Robert Taylor **a.** *Broadway Melody of 1938*; **b.** *Bataan*; **c.** *Billy the Kid*; **d.** *The Gorgeous Hussy*

2. Alice Faye **a.** *That Night in Rio*; **b.** *Lillian Russell*; **c.** *Tin Pan Alley*; **d.** *In Old Chicago*

3. Tyrone Power **a.** *The Mark of Zorro*; **b.** *Marie Antoinette*; **c.** *Lloyd's of London*; **d.** *Jesse James*

4. Marlene Dietrich **a.** *The Flame of New Orleans*; **b.** *Kismet*; **c.** *Golden Earrings*; **d.** *Stage Fright*

5. Fred Astaire **a.** *Broadway Melody of 1940*; **b.** *Holiday Inn*; **c.** *You Were Never Lovelier*; **d.** *Blue Skies*

6. Greer Garson **a.** *Random Harvest*; **b.** *Pride and Prejudice*; **c.** *Blossoms in the Dust*; **d.** *Julius Caesar*

7. Spencer Tracy **a.** *Northwest Passage*; **b.** *Stanley and Livingstone*; **c.** *Captains Courageous*; **d.** *Boom Town*

8. Gene Tierney **a.** *Dragonwyck*; **b.** *Leave Her to Heaven*; **c.** *The Mating Season*; **d.** *Advise and Consent*

9. William Holden **a.** *Dear Ruth*; **b.** *Executive Suite*; **c.** *The Moon Is Blue*; **d.** *Apartment for Peggy*

10. Carole Lombard **a.** *Bolero*; **b.** *The Princess Comes Across*; **c.** *Nothing Sacred*; **d.** *Mr. and Mrs. Smith*

197. Pick the one film in each group in which the performer did **not** appear.

1. Betty Grable
   a. *Down Argentine Way*; b. *Week-End in Havana*;
   c. *Song of the Islands*; d. *Moon Over Miami*

2. Shirley Temple
   a. *Little Miss Broadway*; b. *Poor Little Rich Girl*;
   c. *The Littlest Rebel*; d. *Little Fugitive*

3. Eleanor Powell
   a. *Broadway Melody of 1936*; b. *Broadway Melody of 1938*;
   c. *Broadway Melody of 1940*; d. *Broadway Rhythm*

4. Dick Powell
   a. *The Goldwyn Follies*; b. *Gold Diggers of 1933*;
   c. *Gold Diggers of 1935*; d. *Gold Diggers of 1937*

5. Jean Harlow
   a. *Red-Headed Woman*; b. *Goldie*;
   c. *Blonde Crazy*; d. *Platinum Blonde*

6. Judy Garland
   a. *Andy Hardy Gets Spring Fever*; b. *Love Finds Andy Hardy*;
   c. *Andy Hardy Meets Debutante*; d. *Life Begins for Andy Hardy*

7. Claudette Colbert
   a. *Bride for Sale*; b. *The Bride Comes Home*;
   c. *The Bride Goes Wild*; d. *Guest Wife*

8. Kirk Douglas
   a. *The Big Land*; b. *The Big Sky*;
   c. *The Big Trees*; d. *The Last Sunset*

9. Esther Williams
   a. *Duchess of Idaho*; b. *Texas Carnival*;
   c. *Sun Valley Serenade*; d. *Fiesta*

10. Doris Day
   a. *Tea for Two*; b. *The Best Things in Life Are Free*;
   c. *Lullaby of Broadway*; d. *My Dream Is Yours*

198.   Sometimes big stars make surprise appearances. Match the star to the film in which he/she makes a cameo.

1. Joan Crawford

2. Bing Crosby

3. Robert Taylor

4. Myrna Loy

5. Esther Williams

6. Ava Gardner

7. Burt Lancaster

8. Cary Grant

9. Veronica Lake

10. Marlene Dietrich

a. *Till the Clouds Roll By*

b. *Three Sailors and a Girl*

c. *Without Reservations*

d. *The Princess and the Pirate*

e. *The Band Wagon*

f. *It's a Great Feeling*

g. *Paris When It Sizzles*

h. *I Love Melvin*

i. *The Senator Was Indiscreet*

j. *Hold Back the Dawn*

199.   People often go to the movies in movies. One of the films on the right is watched in one of the films on the left. Match them.

1. *Bonnie and Clyde*

2. *Get Shorty*

3. *Summer of '42*

4. *Radio Days*

5. *Words and Music*

6. *The Purple Rose of Cairo*

7. *L.A. Confidential*

8. *Hannah and Her Sisters*

9. *Twelve Monkeys*

10. *Pennies from Heaven*

a. *Top Hat*

b. *Duck Soup*

c. *Roman Holiday*

d. *Vertigo*

e. *Follow the Fleet*

f. *Camille* (1937)

g. *The Philadelphia Story*

h. *Gold Diggers of 1933*

i. *Now, Voyager*

j. *Touch of Evil*

200.   Match the film about movie people on the left to the fictional film on the right that is part of its story (some of these made-up films are glimpsed and some are just referred to). The clues under the actual films should help a little.

1. **A Star Is Born (1937)**
Vicki Lester's Oscar-winning performance.

a. *The Longest Night*

2. **A Star Is Born (1954)**
Vicki Lester's Oscar-winning performance.

b. *The Doom of the Cat Men*

3. **The Bad and the Beautiful**
One of Jonathan Shields' early films.

c. *Hearts and Pearls*

4. **Singin' in the Rain**
The film that premieres in the first scene.

d. *A World for Two*

5. **Sullivan's Travels**
The director's dream project.

e. *The Fatal Winter*

6. **Silk Stockings**
One of Peggy Dayton's swimming pictures.

f. *O Brother, Where Art Thou?*

7. **What Ever Happened to Baby Jane?**
One of Jane's flops.

g. *Swinging Down to Panama*

8. **The Band Wagon**
One of Tony Hunter's old musicals.

h. *Dream Without End*

9. **The Star**
Margaret Elliot tests for this film.

i. *Neptune's Mother*

10. **Sherlock Jr.**
The film the projectionist enters into.

j. *The Royal Rascal*

The Answers

1. Answers: 1-c, 2-j, 3-h, 4-a, 5-e, 6-g, 7-i, 8-d, 9-f, 10-b

2. Answers: 1-h, 2-b, 3-i, 4-g, 5-a, 6-j, 7-c, 8-e, 9-d, 10-f

3. Answers: 1-c (Gene Tierney), 2-h (Audrey Hepburn), 3-e (no one), 4-a (Rita Hayworth), 5-j (Tippi Hedren), 6-d (Jeanne Crain), 7-i (Leslie Caron), 8-b (Jean Simmons), 9-g (Sue Lyon), 10-f (Jeanne Crain)

4. Answers: 1-b (Gary Cooper), 2-h (James Stewart), 3-e (Joel McCrea), 4-j (Henry Fonda), 5-c (Roland Young), 6-i (James Stewart), 7-f (Walter Huston), 8-d (Colin Clive), 9-g (Gary Cooper), 10-a (Errol Flynn)

5. Answers: 1-e, 2-a, 3-g, 4-f, 5-b, 6-j, 7-d, 8-h, 9-c, 10-i

6. Answers: 1-h, 2-d, 3-f, 4-j, 5-b, 6-e, 7-i, 8-c, 9-a, 10-g

7. Answers: 1-g, 2-e, 3-i, 4-b, 5-c, 6-f, 7-j, 8-d, 9-h, 10-a

8. Answers: 1-h, 2-c, 3-e, 4-a, 5-g, 6-b, 7-i, 8-d, 9-j, 10-f

9. Answers: 1-i, 2-d, 3-a, 4-f, 5-c, 6-j, 7-b, 8-g, 9-e, 10-h

10. Answers: 1-f, 2-a, 3-h, 4-j, 5-d, 6-i, 7-b, 8-g, 9-e, 10-c

11. Answers: 1-c, 2-h, 3-d, 4-a, 5-f, 6-i, 7-j, 8-b, 9-g, 10-e

12. Answers: 1-d (*The Glass Menagerie*), 2-h (*Suddenly, Last Summer*), 3-f (*The Fugitive Kind*), 4-a (*The Roman Spring of Mrs. Stone*), 5-c

(*The Fugitive Kind*), 6-j (*The Night of the Iguana*), 7-b (*The Night of the Iguana*), 8-i (*Sweet Bird of Youth*), 9-e (*Sweet Bird of Youth*), 10-g (*Boom*)

13. Answers: 1-e, 2-h, 3-b, 4-j, 5-g, 6-a, 7-d, 8-i, 9-c, 10-f

14. Answers: 1-e (*Devotion*), 2-i (*Magnificent Doll*), 3-b (*Beloved Infidel*), 4-a (*I Want to Live!*), 5-g (*Young Bess*), 6-j (*Sister Kenny*), 7-h (*The Barretts of Wimpole Street-1957*), 8-f (*The Great Ziegfeld*), 9-c (*The Plainsman*), 10-d (*Sunrise at Campobello*)

15. Answers: 1-g (*The Gorgeous Hussy*), 2-d (*Rembrandt*), 3-j (*Edison, the Man*), 4-e (*Dr. Ehrlich's Magic Bullet*), 5-a (*Juarez*), 6-c (*Viva Villa!*), 7-h (*The Spirit of St. Louis*), 8-b (*The Adventures of Mark Twain*), 9-i (*Story of G.I. Joe*), 10-f (*Magnificent Doll*)

16. Answers: 1-h (the murdered little boy), 2-d (the father's mistress), 3-g (Mary's cheating husband), 4-b (the letter writer), 5-j (the family patriarch), 6-a (the murdered model), 7-e (the beau Blanche is expecting), 8-c (Mrs. Anna's dead husband), 9-f (Brigid's partner-in-crime), 10-i (father of the sextuplets)

17. Answers: 1-h, 2-e, 3-b, 4-j, 5-c, 6-i, 7-a, 8-f, 9-d, 10-g

18. Answers: 1-e (Gregory Peck), 2-d (Joan Crawford), 3-i (Robert Montgomery), 4-b (Carole Lombard), 5-h (Rock Hudson), 6-c (Claudette Colbert), 7-a (May Robson), 8-g (Joel McCrea), 9-f (Jean Arthur), 10-j (Joel McCrea)

19. Answers: 1-g, 2-c, 3-h, 4-f, 5-d, 6-j, 7-e, 8-a, 9-b, 10-i

    Note: Gig Young took his character's name as his professional name. He had been known as Byron Barr.

20. Answers: 1-a, 2-c, 3-d, 4-b, 5-b, 6-a, 7-d, 8-d, 9-b, 10-c

21. Answers: 1-c, 2-h, 3-f, 4-a, 5-j, 6-d, 7-b, 8-e, 9-g, 10-i

22. Answers: 1-e, 2-c, 3-h, 4-a, 5-j, 6-b, 7-i, 8-f, 9-g, 10-d

23. Answers: 1-h, 2-c, 3-j, 4-a, 5-e, 6-b, 7-d, 8-i, 9-g, 10-f

24. Answers: 1-e, 2-h, 3-b, 4-j, 5-a, 6-d, 7-i, 8-f, 9-c, 10-g

25. Answers: 1-d (*The Magnificent Ambersons*), 2-g (*Jezebel*), 3-j (*The Wizard of Oz*), 4-a (*Arsenic and Old Lace*), 5-h (*A Tree Grows in Brooklyn*), 6-c (*The Heiress*), 7-e (*The Little Foxes*), 8-b (*Little Women*), 9-f (*Gone With the Wind*), 10-i (*Oklahoma!*)

26. Answers: 1-e, 2-g, 3-a, 4-f, 5-j, 6-c, 7-i, 8-d, 9-h, 10-b

27. Answers: 1-i (Douglas), 2-d (Stewart), 3-f (Cagney, brother/sister), 4-e (Mills, daughter/father), 5-a (Kerr), 6-b (Barrymore, brothers), 7-h (Taylor), 8-c (Taylor), 9-g (Ladd, father/son), 10-j (Davis)

28. Answers: 1-c, 2-i, 3-d, 4-g, 5-j, 6-f, 7-h, 8-e, 9-a, 10-b

29. Answers: 1-f, 2-i, 3-a, 4-d, 5-g, 6-b, 7-j, 8-e, 9-h, 10-c

30. Answers: 1-f, 2-i, 3-b, 4-a, 5-h, 6-d, 7-j, 8-c, 9-e, 10-g

31. Answers: 1-e, 2-a, 3-d, 4-c, 5-b, 6-j , 7-h, 8-i, 9-f, 10-g

32. Answers: 1-g, 2-f, 3-a, 4-h, 5-c, 6-j, 7-b, 8-d, 9-i, 10-e

33. Answers: 1-i (*The Adventures of Robin Hood*), 2-e (*Anna and the King of Siam*), 3-b (*Robin Hood*), 4-a (*Forever Amber* and *The King's Thief*), 5-g (*The Three Musketeers*), 6-d (*Tower of London*), 7-j (*Knights of the Round Table*), 8-c (*Marie Antoinette*), 9-f (*Becket* and *The Lion in Winter*), 10-h (*Henry V*)

34. Answers: 1-d (*Young Bess*), 2-g (*Adventures of Don Juan*), 3-i (*The Lion in Winter*), 4-a (*Salome*), 5-e (*Rasputin and the Empress*), 6-b (*Fire Over England* and *The Sea Hawk*), 7-j (*Knights of the Round Table*), 8-f (*The Private Life of Henry VIII*), 9-h (*The Mudlark*), 10-c (*The Three Musketeers*)

35. Answers: 1-b (ranch), 2-a (plantation), 3-g (ranch), 4-j (plantation), 5-d (house), 6-c (estate), 7-i (psychiatric institution), 8-e (psychiatric institution), 9-f (fishing lodge), 10-h (estate)

36. Answers: 1-f, 2-j, 3-a, 4-h, 5-c, 6-i, 7-e, 8-d, 9-g, 10-b

37. Answers: 1-c, 2-e, 3-i, 4-f, 5-a, 6-d, 7-j, 8-h, 9-g, 10-b

38. Answers: 1-j, 2-a, 3-e, 4-h, 5-c, 6-i, 7-f, 8-b, 9-g, 10-d

39. Answers: 1-f, 2-i, 3-b, 4-g, 5-a, 6-d, 7-j, 8-h, 9-e, 10-c

40. Answers: 1-i, 2-d, 3-b, 4-f, 5-h, 6-a, 7-e, 8-j, 9-g, 10-c

Note: Lew Ayres was a conscientious objector who served with the Army Medical Corps and also as an assistant chaplain.

41. Answers: 1-e, 2-h, 3-b, 4-j, 5-d, 6-a, 7-c, 8-i, 9-f, 10-g

42. Answers: 1-f, 2-d, 3-i, 4-a, 5-h, 6-j, 7-c, 8-e, 9-g, 10-b

43. Answers: 1-g, 2-e, 3-a, 4-d, 5-h, 6-i, 7-j, 8-b, 9-c, 10-f

44. Answers: 1-e, 2-h, 3-a, 4-d, 5-j, 6-b, 7-c, 8-i, 9-f, 10-g

45. Answers: 1-j, 2-g, 3-b, 4-f, 5-e, 6-a, 7-c, 8-i, 9-d, 10-h

46. Answers: 1-f (Anne Welles), 2-i (title role), 3-e (Susan Alexander), 4-c (Aron Trask), 5-j (title role), 6-h (blind girl), 7-a (Joey Drayton), 8-g (Eddie Kerns), 9-d (Carl Denham), 10-b (Michael Rossi)

47. Answers: 1-d, 2-i, 3-g, 4-e, 5-a, 6-h, 7-b, 8-j, 9-f, 10-c

48. Answers: 1-e, 2-d, 3-a, 4-i, 5-g, 6-c, 7-j, 8-h, 9-b, 10-f

49. Answers: 1-h (*The Public Enemy*), 2-j (*Champion*), 3-d (*Four Daughters*), 4-i (*This Gun for Hire*), 5-b (*Golden Boy*), 6-g (*The Killers*), 7-e (*High Sierra*), 8-a (*Kiss of Death*), 9-c (*East of Eden*), 10-f (*Splendor in the Grass*)

50. Answers: 1-a (*To Have and Have Not*), 2-j (*The Outlaw*), 3-h (*Picnic*), 4-c (*The Killers*), 5-f (*Goodbye, Mr. Chips*), 6-i (*Blood and Sand*), 7-b (*The Jungle Princess*), 8-e (*Intermezzo*), 9-d (*She Done Him Wrong*), 10-g (*Niagara*)

51. Answers: 1-c, 2-f, 3-d, 4-i, 5-b, 6-a, 7-h, 8-e, 9-j, 10-g

52. Answers: 1-i, 2-e, 3-h, 4-a, 5-c, 6-d, 7-j, 8-f, 9-b, 10-g

53. Answers: 1-d, 2-g, 3-b, 4-i, 5-a, 6-c, 7-j, 8-f, 9-e, 10-h

54. Answers: 1-GG (*Anna Karenina*-1935), 2-LG, 3-LG, 4-LG (*The Night of the Hunter*-1955), 5-GG, 6-LG, 7-GG, 8-GG (*Anna Christie*-1930), 9-GG, 10-LG

55. Answers: 1-NS (*The Barretts of Wimpole Street*-1934), 2-GG (*Pride and Prejudice*-1940), 3-NS, 4-NS (*Romeo and Juliet*-1936), 5-GG (*Julius Caesar*-1953), 6-GG (*The Miniver Story*-1950, the sequel to *Mrs. Miniver*-1942), 7-NS, 8-GG (*Blossoms in the Dust*-1941; *Mrs. Miniver*-1942; *Madame Curie*-1943; *Mrs. Parkington*-1944; *The Valley of Decision*-1945), 9-NS, 10-GG

56. Answers: 1-JC, 2-BD (*Of Human Bondage*), 3-JC (*Daisy Kenyon*-1947), 4-BD (*June Bride*), 5-BD, 6-JC (*Mildred Pierce*), 7-JC, 8-BD, 9-BD, 10-JC (*Susan and God*)

57. Answers: 1-JA, 2-CL, 3-CL, 4-JA, 5-CL (*Mr. and Mrs. Smith*), 6-JA (*The Whole Town's Talking*), 7-CL, 8-CL, 9-JA, 10-JA

58. Answers: 1-IL, 2-BS, 3-BS, 4-IL, 5-BS, 6-BS, 7-IL, 8-BS (*Night Nurse*-1931; *To Please a Lady*-1950), 9-IL, 10-IL

59. Answers: 1-JM (same title-1941), 2-JM, 3-AF, 4-JM (*I Married an Angel*), 5-JM (*Bitter Sweet*), 6-AF (*In Old Chicago*-1937), 7-AF, 8-AF, 9-JM, 10-AF

60. Answers: 1-JF, 2-OD, 3-OD (*My Cousin Rachel*), 4-OD, 5-OD (*A Midsummer Night's Dream*-1935), 6-JF, 7-OD, 8-JF, 9-JF (*A Damsel in Distress*-1937), 10-JF (*The Emperor Waltz*-1948, Crosby; *Serenade*-1956, Lanza)

61. Answers: 1-JW, 2-JW (*Stage Fright*), 3-LY (*The Stranger*), 4-LY, 5-LY, 6-JW, 7-LY, 8-JW, 9-LY (*Four Men and a Prayer*-1938; *Three Blind Mice*-1938; *Eternally Yours*-1939; *The Perfect Marriage*-1946; *The Bishop's Wife*-1947), 10-JW (*The Lost Weekend*-1945)

62. Answers: 1-LT (*Honky Tonk*-1941; *Somewhere I'll Find You*-1942; *Homecoming*-1948; *Betrayed*-1954), 2-AG (*The Barefoot Contessa*), 3-LT (*The Bad and the Beautiful*), 4-LT (*The Rains of Ranchipur*), 5-LT (*Week-End at the Waldorf*-1945), 6-AG, 7-AG (*Mogambo*-1953), 8-LT, 9-AG, 10-AG (*One Touch of Venus*-1948)

63. Answers: 1-AH (*Roman Holiday*-1953), 2-AH (*The Nun's Story*-1959), 3-AH (*My Fair Lady*-1964, a remake of *Pygmalion*-1938), 4-GK (*Mogambo*-1953, a remake of *Red Dust*), 5-AH (*Love in the Afternoon*-1957), 6-GK, 7-GK ("True Love" from *High Society*), 8-GK (*Mogambo*-1953), 9-AH (*Roman Holiday*-1953; *The Children's Hour*-1961; *How to Steal a Million*-1966), 10-GK (*The Swan*)

64. Answers: 1-f, 2-c, 3-a, 4-i, 5-d, 6-g, 7-j, 8-b, 9-h, 10-e

65. Answers: 1-d, 2-f, 3-h, 4-a, 5-i, 6-c, 7-e, 8-b, 9-j, 10-g

66. Answers: 1-c, 2-h, 3-f, 4-b, 5-a, 6-i, 7-e, 8-j, 9-g, 10-d

67. Answers: 1-j, 2-e, 3-a, 4-i, 5-g, 6-h, 7-f, 8-b, 9-c, 10-d

68. Answers: 1-j, 2-h, 3-g, 4-f, 5-i, 6-c, 7-d, 8-b, 9-e, 10-a

69. Answers: 1-f, 2-a, 3-h, 4-c, 5-j, 6-e, 7-b, 8-d, 9-i, 10-g

70. Answers: 1-f, 2-b, 3-i, 4-c, 5-a, 6-g, 7-j, 8-d, 9-h, 10-e

71. Answers: 1-h, 2-e, 3-d, 4-g, 5-j, 6-a, 7-f, 8-b, 9-c, 10-i

72. Answers: 1-d, 2-a, 3-i, 4-f, 5-h, 6-c, 7-j, 8-e, 9-b, 10-g

73. Answers: 1-e, 2-h, 3-c, 4-j, 5-a, 6-d, 7-i, 8-f, 9-b, 10-g

74. Answers: 1-a, 2-h, 3-d, 4-i, 5-c, 6-e, 7-j, 8-f, 9-g, 10-b

75. Answers: 1-i, 2-f, 3-h, 4-b, 5-g, 6-j, 7-c, 8-a, 9-e 10-d

76. Answers: 1-b, 2-e, 3-g, 4-a, 5-i, 6-c, 7-j, 8-d, 9-h, 10-f

77. Answers: 1-c, 2-e, 3-d, 4-g, 5-h, 6-j, 7-i, 8-f, 9-a, 10-b

78. Answers: 1-g, 2-c, 3-e, 4-a, 5-i, 6-d, 7-h, 8-b, 9-j, 10-f

79. Answers: 1-g, 2-i, 3-d, 4-b, 5-h, 6-j, 7-e, 8-a, 9-f, 10-c

Note: *That Night in Rio* and *On the Riviera* are both remakes of the 1935 *Folies Bergère* starring Maurice Chevalier.

80. Answers: 1-e, 2-h, 3-a, 4-c, 5-g, 6-b, 7-j, 8-d, 9-f, 10-i

81. Answers: 1-c, 2-g, 3-i, 4-a, 5-j, 6-d, 7-f, 8-e, 9-b, 10-h

82. Answers: 1-g, 2-c, 3-d, 4-i, 5-f, 6-e, 7-a, 8-b, 9-j, 10-h

83. Answers: 1-c, 2-d, 3-j, 4-a, 5-g, 6-i, 7-f, 8-h, 9-b, 10-e

84. Answers: 1-h, 2-e, 3-c, 4-g, 5-i, 6-a, 7-f, 8-j, 9-d, 10-b

85. Answers: 1-b (*Bachelor Mother*; *Magnificent Doll*; *Oh, Men! Oh, Women!*), 2-i (*Phffft*; *Bell, Book and Candle*; *The Notorious Landlady*), 3-e (*Wings in the Dark*; *The Bachelor and the Bobby-Soxer*; *Mr. Blandings Builds His Dream House*), 4-g (*Of Human Bondage*; *The Petrified Forest*; *It's Love I'm After*), 5-d (*Gaslight*; *Arch of Triumph*; *A Matter of Time*), 6-c (*The Stratton Story*; *The Glenn Miller Story*; *Strategic Air Command*), 7-a (*East Side, West Side*; *Pandora and the Flying Dutchman*; *Mayerling*), 8-h (*Crash Drive*; *The Razor's Edge*; *The Luck of the Irish*), 9-j (*Jamaica Inn*; *The Hunchback of Notre Dame*; *This Land is Mine*), 10-f (*Angel Face*; *She Couldn't Say No*; *The Grass is Greener*)

86. Answers: 1-c (*Pillow Talk*; *Lover Come Back*; *Send Me No Flowers*), 2-i (*Woman of the Year*; *Keeper of the Flame*; *Without Love*; *The Sea of Grass*; *State of the Union*; *Adam's Rib*; *Pat and Mike*; *Desk Set*; *Guess Who's Coming to Dinner*), 3-f (*Arabian Nights*; *White Savage*; *Ali Baba and the Forty Thieves*; *Cobra Woman*; *Gypsy Wildcat*; *Sudan*), 4-a (*To Catch a Thief*), 5-h (*Dance, Fools, Dance*; *Laughing Sinners*; *Possessed*; *Dancing Lady*; *Chained*; *Forsaking All Others*; *Love on the Run*; *Strange Cargo*), 6-d (*Next Time We Love*; *The Shopworn Angel*; *The Shop Around the Corner*; *The Mortal Storm*), 7-g (*The Gilded Lily*; *The Bride Comes Home*; *Maid of Salem*; *No Time for Love*; *Practically Yours*; *The Egg and I*; *Family Honeymoon*), 8-b (*The Apartment*; *Irma La Douce*), 9-e (*Ladies in Love*; *Love Is News*; *Café Metropole*; *Second Honeymoon*; *Suez*), 10-j (*Flying Down to Rio*; *The Gay Divorcée*; *Roberta*; *Top Hat*; *Follow the Fleet*; *Swing Time*; *Shall We Dance*; *Carefree*; *The Story of Vernon and Irene Castle*; *The Barkleys of Broadway*)

87. Answers: 1-a, 2-j, 3-h, 4-f, 5-c, 6-i, 7-b, 8-d, 9-g, 10-e

88. Answers: 1-c, 2-a, 3-b, 4-c, 5-a, 6-b, 7-c, 8-d, 9-a, 10-d

Note: Gene Kelly played D'Artagnan in *The Three Musketeers.*

89. Answers: 1-g, 2-d, 3-e, 4-a, 5-c, 6-j, 7-i, 8-f, 9-b, 10-h

90. Answers: 1-g (Irving Berlin), 2-c (Richard Rodgers and Lorenz Hart), 3-h (Jerome Kern and Ira Gershwin), 4-a (Burton Lane and Ralph Freed), 5-j (Cole Porter), 6-b (Irving Berlin), 7-i (George and Ira Gershwin), 8-e (George and Ira Gershwin), 9-d (Harry Warren and Al Dubin), 10-f (Harry Warren and Al Dubin)

91. Answers: 1-a (Harry Warren and Mack Gordon), 2-f (Con Conrad and Herb Magidson), 3-i (Ray Evans and Jay Livingston), 4-g (Ray Evans and Jay Livingston), 5-b (Jerome Kern and Oscar Hammerstein), 6-j (Ralph Rainger and Leo Robin), 7-e (Jerome Kern and Dorothy Fields), 8-d (James Van Heusen and Johnny Burke), 9-c (James Van Heusen and Sammy Cahn), 10-h (Hoagy Carmichael and Johnny Mercer)

92. Answers: 1-d, 2-f, 3-h, 4-a, 5-j, 6-b, 7-e, 8-c, 9-g, 10-i

93. Answers: 1-c, 2-g, 3-a, 4-e, 5-h, 6-f, 7-b, 8-d, 9-j, 10-i

94. Answers: 1-d, 2-g, 3-a, 4-i, 5-c, 6-b, 7-e, 8-f, 9-h, 10-j

95. Answers: 1-h, 2-f, 3-j, 4-b, 5-d, 6-e, 7-a, 8-g, 9-i, 10-c

96. Answers: 1-b, 2-e, 3-i, 4-a, 5-g, 6-d, 7-j, 8-c, 9-h, 10-f

97. Answers: 1-c, 2-e, 3-i, 4-h, 5-j, 6-a, 7-d, 8-g, 9-f, 10-b

98. Answers: 1-c, 2-f, 3-i, 4-a, 5-h, 6-d, 7-e, 8-g, 9-j, 10-b

99. Answers: 1-e, 2-a, 3-h, 4-c, 5-f, 6-i, 7-b, 8-d, 9-g, 10-j

100. Answers: 1-d, 2-g, 3-i, 4-e, 5-j, 6-c, 7-b, 8-a, 9-f, 10-h

101. Answers: 1-g, 2-c, 3-i, 4-e, 5-d, 6-h, 7-a, 8-j, 9-b, 10-f

102. Answers: 1-e, 2-f, 3-b, 4-d, 5-j, 6-c, 7-i, 8-a, 9-g, 10-h

103. Answers: 1-b, 2-i, 3-g, 4-c, 5-h, 6-a, 7-e, 8-j, 9-f, 10-d

104. Answers: 1-d, 2-e, 3-g, 4-i, 5-c, 6-h, 7-j, 8-f, 9-b, 10-a

105. Answers: 1-h, 2-e, 3-b, 4-a, 5-i, 6-d, 7-j, 8-c, 9-g, 10-f

106. Answers: 1-e, 2-c, 3-i, 4-h, 5-f, 6-a, 7-d, 8-j, 9-b, 10-g

107. Answers: 1-d, 2-g, 3-a, 4-j, 5-c, 6-f, 7-i, 8-e, 9-b, 10-h

108. Answers: 1-h (Herman J. Mankiewicz and Orson Welles), 2-e, 3-a (Luise Rainer), 4-j, 5-c (Spencer Tracy), 6-d (John Ford), 7-i (Leo McCarey), 8-g, 9-f, 10-b (Frank Capra)

109. Answers: 1-b, 2-c, 3-b, 4-c, 5-a, 6-a, 7-d, 8-d, 9-b, 10-a

110. Answers: 1-d (1958), 2-d (1964), 3-c (1952), 4-a (1939), 5-b (1943), 6-d (1956), 7-a (1948), 8-b (1945), 9-c (1954), 10-a (1968)

111. Answers: 1-d (1952), 2-a (1942), 3-b (1942), 4-c (1951), 5-b (1946), 6-a (1954), 7-c (1941), 8-d (1945), 9-c (1948), 10-a (1944)

112. Answers: 1-b (1957), 2-a (1953), 3-a (1945), 4-d (1956), 5-c (1936), 6-a (1958), 7-b (1943), 8-c (1945), 9-c (1941), 10-d (1947)

Note: Mitchum and Perkins were nominated in the supporting category.

113. Answers: 1-i (*The Towering Inferno*), 2-j (*Victor/Victoria*), 3-e (*Giant*), 4-b (*Abe Lincoln in Illinois*), 5-a (*The Awful Truth*), 6-d (*Broken Arrow*), 7-c (*A Song to Remember*), 8-h (*Ryan's Daughter*), 9-f (*Sons and Lovers*), 10-g (*The Sand Pebbles*)

Note: Mills was the only winner.

114. Answers: 1-h (*Summer Wishes, Winter Dreams*), 2-g (*Days of Wine and Roses*), 3-d (*Duel in the Sun*), 4-e (*The Blue Veil*), 5-i (*A Passage to India*), 6-b (*The Dark Angel*), 7-j (*The Whales of August*), 8-c (*Our Town*), 9-a (*Morocco*), 10-f (*Baby Doll*)

Note: Ashcroft was the only winner.

115. Answers: 1-d (1942), 2-i (1936), 3-b (1930-31), 4-h (1932-33), 5-j (1950), 6-g (1967), 7-a (1944), 8-e (1943), 9-c (1954), 10-f (1934)

Note: Lukas was the only winner.

116. Answers: 1-c (*Gaslight*-1944), 2-g (*The Miracle Worker*-1962), 3-j (*The Country Girl*-1954), 4-e (*Guess Who's Coming to Dinner*-1967), 5-b (*Come Back, Little Sheba*-1952), 6-i (*On the Waterfront*-1954), 7-a (*Butterfield 8*-1960), 8-d (*It Happened One Night*-1934), 9-f (*The Heiress*-1949), 10-h (*Written on the Wind*-1956)

Note: Malone and Saint won in the supporting category.

117. Answers: 1-j (1941), 2-d (1966), 3-f (1959), 4-e (1955), 5-c (1963), 6-a (1945), 7-b (1950), 8-i (1948), 9-h (1929-30), 10-g (1949)

118. Answers: 1-h (1948), 2-a (1957), 3-f (1950), 4-c (1927-28), 5-i (1940), 6-e (1932-33), 7-b (1935), 8-j (1947), 9-d (1945), 10-g (1929-30)

119. Answers: 1-e (*Suspicion*-1941), 2-c (*Kentucky*-1938), 3-h (*Goodbye, Mr. Chips*-1969; Robert Donat won in 1939), 4-f (*Sabrina*), 5-a (1941 nomination for *Hold Back the Dawn*, but lost to Joan Fontaine in *Suspicion*), 6-g (*Abe Lincoln in Illinois*-1940; Daniel Massey was nominated for his Noël Coward in *Star!*-1968), 7-i (*Champion*-1949; *Bright Victory*-1951; *Trial*-1955; *Peyton Place*-1957; all directed by Mark Robson), 8-d (*The Happy Ending*-1969; directed by Richard Brooks), 9-j (Henry VIII in *Anne of the Thousand Days*-1969; Laughton won for *The Private Life of Henry VIII*-1932-33), 10-b (*Summertime*-1955)

120. Answers: 1-d (*Lovely to Look At*), 2-e (*An Affair to Remember*), 3-j (*Always*), 4-a (*Let's Do It Again*), 5-c (*Move Over, Darling*), 6-h (same title), 7-i (same title), 8-g (*Interlude*), 9-f (same title), 10-b (same title)

121. Answers: 1-c, 2-f, 3-i, 4-a, 5-e, 6-j, 7-d, 8-b, 9-h, 10-g

122. Answers: 1-g, 2-h, 3-i, 4-a, 5-e, 6-c, 7-j, 8-b, 9-d, 10-f

123. Answers: 1-i (*Two Girls on Broadway*), 2-f (same title), 3-d (*Congo Maisie*), 4-e (*Easy to Wed*), 5-j (same title), 6-g (*Satan Met a Lady*), 7-b (same title), 8-a (*Castle on the Hudson*), 9-h (same title), 10-c (*A Place in the Sun*)

124. Answers: 1-d (*The Barretts of Wimpole Street*), 2-a (*A Star Is Born*), 3-h (*Pygmalion/My Fair Lady*), 4-b (*Goodbye, Mr. Chips*), 5-g (*The

Philadelphia Story/High Society), 6-c (*Ninotchka/Silk Stockings*), 7-e (*Red Dust/Mogambo*), 8-f (*Mutiny on the Bounty*), 9-i (*The Shop Around the Corner/In the Good Old Summertime*), 10-j (*The Champ*)

125. Answers: 1-e (*Walk, Don't Run*), 2-h (*The Life and Times of Judge Roy Bean*), 3-a (same title), 4-c (Cisco Kid series), 5-j (*High Society*), 6-g (*The Mudlark*), 7-d (*The Girl Who Had Everything*), 8-f (*A Man for All Seasons*), 9-b (*You Can't Run Away from It*), 10-i (same title)

126. Answers: 1-b, 2-e, 3-j, 4-g, 5-c, 6-i, 7-a, 8-d, 9-f, 10-h

127. Answers: 1-f (*Summer Holiday*), 2-c (*A Song Is Born*), 3-i (*You Can't Run Away From It*), 4-a (*Bundle of Joy*), 5-j (*The Girl Most Likely*), 6-d (*Masquerade in Mexico*), 7-g (*Three for the Show*), 8-e (*I'll Be Yours*), 9-b (*About Face*), 10-h (*The Chocolate Soldier*)

Note: MGM replaced the *Arms and the Man* plot with *The Guardsman*'s plot when they made *The Chocolate Soldier* into a film.

128. Answers: 1-f, 2-h, 3-b, 4-a, 5-c, 6-j, 7-e, 8-d, 9-i, 10-g

129. Answers: 1-d, 2-f, 3-b, 4-i, 5-a, 6-h, 7-j, 8-e, 9-g, 10-c

130. Answers: 1-f (*Mrs. Miniver/The Miniver Story*), 2-d (*Father of the Bride/Father's Little Dividend*), 3-j (Dr. Kildare series) 4-a (Andy Hardy series), 5-h (*Boys Town/Men of Boys Town*), 6-g (*Jesse James/The Return of Frank James*), 7-b (*Dear Ruth/Dear Wife*), 8-c (*The Thin Man* series), 9-e (*See Here, Private Hargrove/What Next, Corporal Hargrove?*), 10-i (*On Moonlight Bay/By the Light of the Silvery Moon*)

131. Answers: 1-a, 2-g, 3-e, 4-j, 5-b, 6-d, 7-h, 8-f, 9-c, 10-i

132. Answers: 1-i, 2-e, 3-b, 4-g, 5-a, 6-c, 7-j, 8-f, 9-d, 10-h

133. Answers: 1-e (team), 2-c (LeRoy replaced Ford), 3-i (team), 4-a (team), 5-h (team), 6-j (team), 7-b (Wyler replaced Hawks), 8-d (team), 9-g (team), 10-f (Curtiz replaced Keighley)

134. Answers: 1-e, 2-j, 3-g, 4-b, 5-i, 6-a, 7-f, 8-d, 9-h, 10-c

135. Answers: 1-i, 2-f, 3-e, 4-g, 5-a, 6-c, 7-h, 8-j, 9-d, 10-b

136. Answers: 1-d (*Sunset Boulevard*; *Stalag 17*; *Sabrina*; *Fedora*), 2-g (*Romance on the High Seas*; *My Dream Is Yours*; *Young Man With a Horn*; *I'll See You in My Dreams*), 3-j (*The Plainsman*; *North West Mounted Police*; *The Story of Dr. Wassell*; *Unconquered*), 4-f (*Babes in Arms*; *Strike Up the Band*; *Babes on Broadway*; *For Me and My Gal*), 5-h (*The Ghost and Mrs. Muir*; *Escape*; *Cleopatra*; *The Honey Pot*), 6-i (*Man Hunt*; *The Woman in the Window*; *Scarlet Street*; *Secret Beyond the Door*), 7-c (*Rope*; *Rear Window*; *The Man Who Knew Too Much*; *Vertigo*), 8-a (*Ladies of Leisure*; *The Miracle Woman*; *Forbidden*; *The Bitter Tea of General Yen*; *Meet John Doe*), 9-b (*These Three*; *The Heiress*; *Carrie*; *The Children's Hour*), 10-e (*The Love Parade*; *Monte Carlo*; *One Hour With You*; *The Merry Widow*)

Note: James Stewart and Frank Capra made only 3 films together.

137. Answers: 1-d, 2-j, 3-h, 4-b, 5-e, 6-a, 7-i, 8-g, 9-c, 10-f

138. Answers: 1-d, 2-j, 3-b, 4-g, 5-i, 6-c, 7-a, 8-f, 9-h, 10-e

139. Answers: 1-g, 2-e, 3-h, 4-i, 5-f, 6-b, 7-a, 8-d, 9-c, 10-j

140. Answers: 1-j, 2-e, 3-h, 4-b, 5-d, 6-a, 7-i, 8-c, 9-f, 10-g

141. Answers: 1-f, 2-g, 3-i, 4-a, 5-h, 6-b, 7-d, 8-j, 9-c, 10-e

142. Answers: 1-c, 2-e, 3-i, 4-a, 5-b, 6-g, 7-j, 8-f, 9-d, 10-h

143. Answers: 1-c, 2-f, 3-i, 4-a, 5-d, 6-h, 7-b, 8-j, 9-e, 10-g

144. Answers: 1-a, 2-e, 3-h, 4-c, 5-b, 6-j, 7-f, 8-d, 9-g, 10-i

145. Answers: 1-e, 2-d, 3-i, 4-b, 5-g, 6-c, 7-j, 8-a, 9-f, 10-h

146. Answers: 1-e, 2-d, 3-i, 4-g, 5-a, 6-j, 7-c, 8-f, 9-b, 10-h

147. Answers: 1-d, 2-h, 3-f, 4-b, 5-j, 6-e, 7-i, 8-c, 9-g, 10-a

148. Answers: 1-c, 2-f, 3-g, 4-a, 5-e, 6-b, 7-i, 8-j, 9-d, 10-h

149. Answers: 1-d (Cliff Robertson), 2-f (Gene Tierney), 3-b (Katharine Hepburn-1932; Maureen O'Hara-1940), 4-a (Joan Crawford), 5-h (Gregory Peck), 6-j (Joanne Woodward), 7-e (Olivia de Havilland), 8-g (Katharine Hepburn), 9-c (Claude Rains), 10-i (Anthony Perkins)

150. Answers: 1-f (Florence Bates), 2-i (Jessie Royce Landis), 3-e (Elizabeth Taylor), 4-j (Marlene Dietrich), 5-g (Ida Lupino), 6-h (Audrey Hepburn), 7-a (Paul Henreid), 8-c (Horst Buchholz), 9-b (Robert Walker), 10-d (William Holden)

151. Answers: 1-e (Elizabeth Taylor), 2-g (Tallulah Bankhead), 3-f (Lana Turner), 4-b (Priscilla Lane), 5-i (Ann Dvorak), 6-c (Piper Laurie), 7-a (Marlene Dietrich), 8-j (Lana Turner), 9-h (James Mason), 10-d (Angela Scoular)

152. Answers: 1-f, 2-c, 3-a, 4-i, 5-g, 6-e, 7-j, 8-b, 9-h, 10-d

153. Answers: 1-g, 2-i (curtain call), 3-b, 4-f, 5-a, 6-j, 7-d, 8-h, 9-c, 10-e

154. Answers: 1-f (with Jane Murfin), 2-c (with John Huston), 3-h (with Alan Campbell and Robert Carson), 4-b (with Albert Hackett and Frances Goodrich), 5-j, 6-a (with Tennessee Williams), 7-i (with Edward E. Paramore), 8-e (with Jules Furthman), 9-g, 10-d (with John Huston)

155. Answers: 1-b (Irene Dunne), 2-d (Gene Tierney), 3-g (Auriol Lee), 4-i (Rosalind Russell), 5-a (Charles Boyer), 6-j (Dick Powell), 7-e (Cary Grant), 8-f (the murdered doctor), 9-c (Oscar Homolka), 10-h (Miriam Hopkins)

156. Answers: 1-g, 2-d, 3-i, 4-a, 5-j, 6-e, 7-c, 8-h, 9-b, 10-f

157. Answers: 1-CC, 2-CC (*The Circus*-1927-28), 3-BK, 4-BK, 5-CC, 6-CC (*The Great Dictator*-1940), 7-BK, 8-BK, 9-CC (*Monsieur Verdoux*), 10-BK

158. Answers: 1-HB (*The African Queen*-1951), 2-EGR, 3-HB, 4-HB (*The Petrified Forest*), 5-EGR (*The Woman in the Window*-1944; *Scarlet Street*-1945), 6-EGR (*The Stranger*-1946), 7-EGR, 8-HB, 9-EGR, 10-HB (*Dead End*-1937; *The Desperate Hours*-1955)

159. Answers: 1-ST, 2-CG, 3-CG (*The Misfits*-1961), 4-CG, 5-CG, 6-ST, 7-ST, 8-ST (*The Sea of Grass*-1947), 9-ST, 10-CG

160. Answers: 1-JS, 2-CG (*Once Upon a Honeymoon*-1942; *Monkey Business*-1952), 3-CG, 4-JS, 5-CG, 6-JS (*Rose Marie*-1936), 7-CG (*North by Northwest*-1959), 8-JS, 9-JS, 10-CG (*The Talk of the Town*)

161. Answers: 1-TP, 2-TP, 3-EF, 4-EF, 5-TP, 6-TP, 7-EF, 8-EF, 9-EF, 10-TP

162. Answers: 1-JM (*Colorado Territory*-1949), 2-RS (*Roberta*-1935; *Follow the Fleet*-1936), 3-RS, 4-JM, 5-JM, 6-RS (*The Spoilers* and *Pittsburgh*), 7-JM, 8-RS, 9-JM, 10-RS

163. Answers: 1-GK, 2-GK (*Les Girls*-1957), 3-FA (*Finian's Rainbow*-1968), 4-GK (*The Three Musketeers*), 5-FA (*Yolanda and the Thief*-1945), 6-FA ("The Way You Look Tonight" from *Swing Time*-1936), 7-GK (*For Me and My Gal*-1942), 8-FA (*Royal Wedding*-1951), 9-FA (*Daddy Long Legs*), 10-GK

164. Answers: 1-AG, 2-AG, 3-LO, 4-AG, 5-AG, 6-LO, 7-LO, 8-AG, 9-LO (*Spartacus*), 10-LO

165. Answers: 1-KD (*Ace in the Hole*), 2-BL (*Trapeze*-1956; *Sweet Smell of Success*-1957), 3-BL, 4-KD (*The Strange Love of Martha Ivers*-1946), 5-KD, 6-KD (*The Bad and the Beautiful*-1952; *Lust for Life*-1956; *Two Weeks in Another Town*-1962), 7-BL (*Elmer Gantry*-1960), 8-BL (*The Unforgiven*), 9-BL, 10-KD

166. Answers: 1-MC (*Indiscretion of an American Wife*), 2-MB (*A Countess from Hong Kong*-1967), 3-MC (*I Confess*-1953), 4-MC (*Red River*-1948), 5-MB (*The Men*-1950), 6-MB (*Bedtime Story*-1964), 7-MC (*From Here to Eternity*), 8-MB (*On the Waterfront*), 9-MC (*The Misfits*), 10-MB

167. Answers: 1-d, 2-f, 3-i, 4-g, 5-h, 6-b, 7-a, 8-e, 9-j, 10-c

168. Answers: 1-c, 2-h, 3-a, 4-g, 5-d, 6-b, 7-i, 8-f, 9-j, 10-e

169. Answers: 1-c, 2-a, 3-h, 4-b, 5-j, 6-e, 7-d, 8-i, 9-g, 10-f

170. Answers: 1-f (*Dancing Lady*), 2-c (*Broadway Melody of 1940*), 3-b

(*Ziegfeld Follies*), 4-j (*Easter Parade*), 5-i (*You Were Never Lovelier*), 6-a (*Swing Time*), 7-d (*Daddy Long Legs*), 8-g (*Royal Wedding*), 9-h (*Silk Stockings*), 10-e (*Funny Face*)

171. Answers: 1-a (*Anchors Aweigh*), 2-i (*Brigadoon*), 3-b (*Cover Girl*), 4-e (*Singin' in the Rain*), 5-g (*It's Always Fair Weather*), 6-h (*An American in Paris*), 7-j (*Deep in My Heart*), 8-d (*Ziegfeld Follies*), 9-c (*Anchors Aweigh*), 10-f (*Cover Girl*)

172. Answers: 1-f, 2-e, 3-h, 4-j, 5-c, 6-b, 7-d, 8-g, 9-a, 10-i

173. Answers: 1-f, 2-h, 3-e, 4-b, 5-i, 6-a, 7-d, 8-c, 9-j, 10-g

174. Answers: 1-f, 2-j, 3-e, 4-h, 5-a, 6-g, 7-i, 8-d, 9-b, 10-c

175. Answers: 1-g, 2-a, 3-f, 4-i, 5-j, 6-b, 7-e, 8-d, 9-h, 10-c

176. Answers: 1-e, 2-d, 3-j, 4-g, 5-c, 6-h, 7-a, 8-b, 9-i, 10-f

177. Answers: 1-c, 2-f, 3-g, 4-j, 5-b, 6-e, 7-i, 8-h, 9-a, 10-d

178. Answers: 1-i, 2-h, 3-e, 4-c, 5-f, 6-j, 7-g, 8-b, 9-a, 10-d

179. Answers: 1-g, 2-d, 3-b, 4-i, 5-c, 6-e, 7-a, 8-f, 9-h, 10-j

180. Answers: 1-e, 2-c, 3-i, 4-f, 5-h, 6-a, 7-d, 8-j, 9-g, 10-b

181. Answers: 1-g, 2-a, 3-j, 4-f, 5-h, 6-i, 7-b, 8-c, 9-d, 10-e

182. Answers: 1-f, 2-i, 3-a, 4-d, 5-g, 6-e, 7-b, 8-j, 9-c, 10-h

183. Answers: 1-c, 2-j, 3-f, 4-d, 5-b, 6-e, 7-a, 8-h, 9-g, 10-i

184. Answers: 1-c, 2-g, 3-j, 4-i, 5-f, 6-b, 7-a, 8-e, 9-h, 10-d

185. Answers: 1-b, 2-d, 3-g, 4-a, 5-c, 6-j, 7-i, 8-h, 9-e, 10-f

186. Answers: 1-d, 2-a, 3-i, 4-f, 5-h, 6-c, 7-e, 8-j, 9-b, 10-g

187. Answers: 1-i (directed by Luchino Visconti), 2-d (directed by Jean-Luc Godard), 3-h (directed by Luchino Visconti), 4-f (directed by Roberto Rossellini), 5-j (directed by Federico Fellini), 6-b (directed by Michelangelo Antonioni), 7-e (directed by Jean-Luc Godard),

8-c (directed by Jean Renoir), 9-a (directed by Federico Fellini), 10-g (directed by G.W. Pabst)

188. Answers: 1-j, 2-g, 3-a, 4-f, 5-d, 6-i, 7-b, 8-c, 9-h, 10-e

189. Answers: 1-i (story), 2-f (based on her and Larry Marcus' story), 3-b (based on his original story), 4-a (screenplay), 5-j (screenplay), 6-d (screenplay with Garson Kanin), 7-c (screenplay), 8-g (screenplay with Collier Young), 9-h (his and Gene Kelly's story), 10-e (story idea)

190. Answers: 1-e, 2-g, 3-i, 4-d, 5-c, 6-j, 7-b, 8-a, 9-f, 10-h

191. Answers: 1-g, 2-c, 3-i, 4-a, 5-h, 6-d, 7-j, 8-b, 9-e, 10-f

Note: Dassin and Leisen also directed. Cole also choreographed.

192. Answers: 1-g, 2-d, 3-i, 4-b, 5-h, 6-a, 7-e, 8-j, 9-c, 10-f

193. Answers: 1-c, 2-g, 3-h, 4-f, 5-j, 6-i, 7-a, 8-d, 9-e, 10-b

194. Answers: 1-f (*W.C. Fields and Me*), 2-c (*Man of a Thousand Faces*), 3-h (*Chaplin*), 4-a (*The Jolson Story/Jolson Sings Again*), 5-g (*Too Much, Too Soon*), 6-d (*The George Raft Story*), 7-j (*The Buster Keaton Story*), 8-b (*The Eddie Cantor Story*), 9-e (*Ed Wood*), 10-i (*Gable and Lombard*)

195. Answers: 1-c, 2-b, 3-a, 4-d, 5-c, 6-a, 7-d, 8-b, 9-b, 10-c

196. Answers: 1-c, 2-a, 3-d, 4-b, 5-d, 6-c, 7-a, 8-b, 9-d, 10-c

197. Answers: 1-b, 2-d, 3-d, 4-a, 5-c, 6-a, 7-c, 8-a, 9-c, 10-b

198. Answers: 1-f, 2-d, 3-h, 4-i, 5-a, 6-e, 7-b, 8-c, 9-j, 10-g

199. Answers: 1-h, 2-j, 3-i, 4-g, 5-f, 6-a, 7-c, 8-b, 9-d, 10-e

200. Answers: 1-h (Janet Gaynor), 2-d (Judy Garland), 3-b (Kirk Douglas), 4-j, 5-f (Joel McCrea), 6-i (Janis Paige), 7-a (Bette Davis), 8-g (Fred Astaire), 9-e (Bette Davis), 10-c (Buster Keaton)

Score Card

Points	How Well Did You Do?
0-250	**"Sorry, Wrong Number"** —It's okay to admit that the only pre-1970 movies you really care about are *The Wizard of Oz* and *It's a Wonderful Life*.
250-500	**"To Each His Own"** —You probably prefer color to black-and-white, but you do acknowledge that *All About Eve* and *On the Waterfront* are great movies.
500-750	**"The Road to Glory"** —Nobody has to tell you who Ida Lupino is.
750-1000	**"Good News"** —You know your stuff, but still can't tell the difference between Arlene Dahl and Rhonda Fleming.
1000-1250	**"It's a Gift"** —You tend to record a lot of movies off the TV each week. So much DVR space, so little time.
1250-1500	**"Sweet Smell of Success"** —Impressive. You certainly mourn the fact that Ann Sheridan didn't get better roles after proving herself in *Kings Row*.
1500-1750	**"Magnificent Obsession"** —Bravo. You'd rather watch old movies than take a walk in the park on the most beautiful day of the year. You pretend to feel guilty about it.
1750-2000+	**"As Good As It Gets"** —Move over Gable and Loy, as you are now the new King or Queen of Hollywood. You deserve a star on the Walk of Fame, your footprints in cement, and immediate employment as head of a major studio.

Other Books by John DiLeo

from Hansen Publishing Group

Spanning titles and eras from *The Student Prince in Old Heidelberg* (1927) to *Three Kings* (1999), ***Screen Savers: 40 Remarkable Movies Awaiting Rediscovery*** by John DiLeo is not the typical collection of nostalgia-minded movie reviews. DiLeo provides such detailed analyses and enlightening critiques that readers will finish the book eager to view all of the forty films featured in his third and latest book. Moviegoers of all persuasions will discover fresh spins on the careers of famous stars and new insights into the screen's essential genres.

Tennessee Williams and Company: His Essential Screen Actors takes a critical look at eleven actors and their roles, bonded by their sustained artistic and professional association with Tennessee Williams, specifically the success, and sometimes failure, of their interpretations of his characters for the screen. The results include some of the more remarkable performances in movie history, from Marlon Brando and Vivien Leigh in *A Streetcar Named Desire* to Anna Magnani in *The Rose Tattoo* and Geraldine Page in *Sweet Bird of Youth*.

Screen Savers II is John DiLeo's three-part grab bag of classic movies, beginning with his extensive essays about ten remarkable and underappreciated movies, representing a variety of genres. Part Two collects and categorizes posts from DiLeo's classic-film blog screensaversmovies.com. Part Three might be called a delayed bonus round to DiLeo's 1999 quiz book, with all-new matching quizzes.

About the Author

 John DiLeo's first book was *And You Thought You Knew Classic Movies!* (St. Martin's, 1999), hailed by Pauline Kael as "the smartest movie quiz book I've ever seen." His second book was *100 Great Film Performances You Should Remember—But Probably Don't* (Limelight Editions, 2002), which Adolph Green called "a valuable and touching work." TCM host Robert Osborne said, in the *Hollywood Reporter,* that the book "delightfully throws the spotlight on some remarkable film work," and the *Washington Post*'s reaction was, "Not only is this helpful criticism, but *100 Great Film Performances* can serve as balm for anyone who has ever been disgruntled by the Academy's choices on Oscar night." Turner Classic Movies devoted a night of prime-time programming to films featured in John's third book, *Screen Savers: 40 Remarkable Movies Awaiting Rediscovery* (Hansen Publishing Group, 2007). His fourth film book, *Tennessee Williams and Company: His Essential Screen Actors* (Hansen Publishing Group, 2010), led to his presentations and panels at the Tennessee Williams festivals in Provincetown and New Orleans. *Show Business Weekly* called John's fifth book, *Screen Savers II: My Grab Bag of Classic Movies*, "witty, clever and perceptive" and "a must for movie buffs." Essays by him appear in two anthologies, *City Secrets Movies: The Ultimate Insider's Guide* (2009) and *City Secrets Books: The Essential Insider's Guide* (2009). John has been a contributing book reviewer for the *Washington Post* and currently writes DVD and film-book reviews for multiple publications. He frequently hosts classic-film series, appears on radio programs, lectures on cruise ships, conducts film-history seminars, and has been an annual participant in the Black Bear Film Festival (Milford, PA) where he interviewed Farley Granger (2005), Arlene Dahl (2006), and Marge Champion (2010) on the festival's stage. His website is johndileo.com and his blog is screensaversmovies.com. Born in 1961 in Brooklyn, John was raised on Long Island and graduated from Ithaca College in 1982 with a B.F.A. After twenty-seven years together, he married partner Earl McCarroll in 2009 in Massachusetts.